From the time when Nicole B. Simpson was a young girl, she knew exactly what she wanted from life and how she was going to get it. Her spirit and passion are what set her apart from her colleagues. She has taken a monotonous subject of finances and turned it into a spiritual journey filled with good humor, real life events and a blueprint for financial security. *The Ultimate Plan: A Financial Survival Guide for Life's Unexpected Events* is a "must have" read!

Sonji Grandy, Smoovegearinc.com

Nicole Simpson has been a contributing columnist with our online publication since its inception. Her astute and practical insight, not only in areas of finance, but with people, is what makes her an invaluable gem to this generation. Within each page of her timely book, there is the sense that she cares about the reader. That kind of "heart and soul" approach can't be taught in a licensing course. It is acquired when you have walked through the corridors of life and experienced certain lessons firsthand. This book is sure to become a handbook and a roadmap for those who need to navigate through life on purpose, with purpose.

Gil Michel, President of BlackMoneyMatters.com

The Ultimate Plan: A Financial Survival Guide for Life's Unexpected Events, by Nicole B. Simpson, is an insightful guide for successful financial planning. The advice offered in this book is timeless and presents realistic options not only for retirement, but for disaster preparation as well. The author's experience as a September 11 survivor—and her subsequent epiphany regarding family provisions—both captivates and compels the reader to begin to map out and then implement a plan of action in the event of any unexpected catastrophe. As a baby boomer, the information on retirement planning is invaluable to me. Yet the financial principles outlined in the book are equally relevant for my mother and my adult daughter. This is a must-read handbook across generations for these uncertain times.

Juanita Fortune, Director, Diamonds and
Pearls Mentoring and Abstinence Program

"Powerful! Impactful! In the wake of wars, recessions, job layoffs, downsizing and natural disasters, Nicole has provided an easy to read and understandable guide to avoiding personal and financial disaster. *The Ultimate Plan* is a must read for anyone who is serious about preparing for their future."

Stephanie L. Jones, Author of *The Enemy Between My Legs,* Detroit, MI

"As the publisher of a start up venture, Nicole's wealth of financial knowledge has allowed me to develop a plan of action that is allowing my business to grow into the business God ordained it to be. I have been blessed to know such a wonderful woman!"

Angelia L. White
Publisher/CEO
Hope for Women Magazine

Minister Nicole B. Simpson is a woman of God with integrity and excellence who has a mandate on her life to reach people from all walks of life to change their life for the rest of their life.

Minister Simpson is dedicated to changing lives and building communities with her many years of knowledge as a Certified Financial Planner. Her book *The Ultimate Plan: A Financial Survival Guide for Life's Unexpected Events* will equip you on how to disciple your life for managing your finance now and for retirement. Our life has changed 180 degrees since we applied the principles. I recommend this book without hesitation and challenge you to read this book and buy it for a friend.

Pastor John E. Blacknall, Founding Pastor/
President of Rhema Word Ministries

"Nicole Simpson has taken on a subject we all fear but must face. She is a gifted servant of the Lord and uniquely qualified to spread the gospel of financial planning and disaster preparation. She gets an 'A' from me!"

Tim Espar
Department of Journalism and Media Studies
Rutgers University

The Ultimate Plan: A Financial Survival Guide for Life's Unexpected Events provides a realistic, easy-to-follow, appealing roadmap for anyone with the common question, "Where shall I begin?" Nicole does a phenomenal job of approaching financial planning with real life examples and providing the tools required to manage all aspects of finances. If you desire to have a solid financial plan and need direction of where to begin, this should be the book you read next.

Vashti Encarnacion, Founder, Faith-Full Foundations

"Nicole B. Simpson has a real heart for the African American community and any community that does not understand biblical standards for living an abundant life. I met Nicole in March of 2004 via a phone call to WRSU FM, New Brunswick. I called to invite her to speak to the women of Edna Mahan Correctional Facility in Clinton, NJ. Nicole was enthusiastic and said that she would be honored to speak. Imagine a stranger being eager to speak to women in prison! She not only spoke to over 100 women on April 20, 2004, she provided 11 of my students with copies of her first book *The Ultimate Plan.* Nicole wrote a short note with an accompanying Bible verse to each one of my students on their personal copy of the books she brought to the prison. I was very moved by her generous gesture. Each inscription that Nicole wrote was inspirational to my students. They will never forget her and her advice to them. Nicole has graciously donated her busy time in the following years to speak to the women about getting financially fit. She did initially tell some of her personal story to the inmates. When she did this, it personally 'blew me away!' The women could really relate to her and her story. Nicole and I have prayed together, talked together, hoped together for women in need, counseled together, and loved our Lord and Savior Jesus Christ together. She is a friend and woman I admire. I can say it is a privilege to know Nicole B. Simpson in this lifetime and hereafter."

Jane Pursell, Edna Mahan Correctional
Facility for Women Education Department

THE
ULTIMATE
PLAN

THE
ULTIMATE
PLAN

A FINANCIAL
SURVIVAL GUIDE
FOR LIFE'S
UNEXPECTED EVENTS

NICOLE B. SIMPSON, CFP®

TATE PUBLISHING & *Enterprises*

Published by Tate Publishing & Enterprises, LLC
127 E. Trade Center Terrace | Mustang, Oklahoma 73064 USA
1.888.361.9473 | www.tatepublishing.com

Tate Publishing is committed to excellence in the publishing industry. The company reflects the philosophy established by the founders, based on Psalm 68:11,
"The Lord gave the word and great was the company of those who published it."

Book design copyright © 2007 by Tate Publishing, LLC. All rights reserved.
Cover & Interior design by Isaiah R. McKee

Published in the United States of America

ISBN: 978-1-60462-495-3
1. Christian Living: Practical Life 2. Personal Finance

08.01.10

DEDICATION

To my heavenly Father, who prepared me to tell this story from experience. To my husband, Jesse, who lived through disaster with me. To my two wonderful children, Jesse and Emani, who I could draw strength from their presence. To every individual who will read this book and decide today is the day to develop "The Ultimate Plan."

ACKNOWLEDGEMENTS

I would like to take this time out to say a special thank you to my husband, Jesse, my first pastor, who has the monumental task of shepherding me. To my prayer partner, Stephanie L. Jones, who holds me accountable to the voice of God and His assignment for my life. To my spiritual parents, Pastor John E. Blacknall and Evangelist Beverly Allen, because of your wisdom, guidance, unconditional support and love. To my family at Rhema Word Ministries—special thanks to Lady Michelle for helping me to realize my worth, and Elder Thomas Blacknall, who joined me in the prayer circle.

Without my experience at Edna Mahan Correctional Facilities for Women, I would not fully appreciate disaster planning—thank you. To Juanita Fortune, you made me sound intelligent. For every individual who contributed to this book and validated my expertise through their personal testimony. To my mother, Wilma, for giving birth to me, my sisters, Anita and Tanya, because whenever I call you, you answer. A special thank you to my sister, Sonji, who provided quail when I only had manna during my wilderness experience. May God bless your seeds sown.

Finally, thank you Tate Publishing for lining up with the vision and assisting me with making this dream a reality.

TABLE OF CONTENTS

FOREWORD

At a period of time when I thought my wife passed away because of the tragedy of 9/11, what immediately came to mind was how was I going to exist without her, how would I raise my children without a mother, how was I going to survive. Financial stability or instability never entered into the picture-I was emotionally affected. I speak from a family's point of view when I state, money is not a primary thought. Personally, upon reflection, I was comforted with knowing that we had a survival plan in place should we ever encounter premature death.

The greatest lesson I've learned during these last several years has humbled me because I realized that even with the best laid out plans, life happens. People die, people lose jobs, people separate, people start over, and people lose everything. What separated our family from others is the belief that we could start over, even in the midst of the storm.

Having a life plan is critical and in my opinion, one cannot avoid taking the necessary steps to ensure financial stability during the different seasons in life. Everyone should take a step back and evaluate where they are standing periodically to ensure they have the greatest opportunity to move forward in life.

Even in the midst of the storm we encountered during this last season, my dependency upon God has always comforted me in knowing that I am a survivor for I know that He is always with me. This book, The Ultimate Plan …is a result of our personal life journey helping us to realize that life happens.

I encourage every individual who desires for their life to be different, to take action immediately and follow through on the plan you put in place. The opportunity to get your life in order can only be fully maximized if you take action.

Jesse L. Simpson III

INTRODUCTION

I began to evaluate my life when I turned thirty years old in January 2001. I knew that God had called me for a purpose and that purpose was to be a Minister of Finance. I did not know exactly what that meant, but I envisioned a young lady speaking to crowds of people, teaching them about money. They would learn how to earn money, how to manage money, and ultimately how to keep money. That young lady would also serve to educate, empower, and enlighten the youth and the churches. Being that young lady, I knew my culture needed economic empowerment.

The African American community finally has the resources and the ability to make a change in our community. The Hip Hop culture has broadened the opportunity to think and grow rich. The ability to rap and break dance gave many teenagers a glimmer of hope that they too could reach beyond their surroundings to find success in business. It has given us the power we needed on a corporate level to make a significant difference. Unfortunately, many of us do not know how to get started.

My knowledge and expertise were in place, but what I envisioned and where I was were two different things. My clientele as a certified financial planner consisted mostly of entertainers, corporate personnel, and small business owners. My calling was crystal clear. However, a change was needed in order to fulfill what God has called for me to do.

At the age of thirty, I was in a partnership with a major financial institution earning over $100,000 a year, working an average of seventy hours a week in an uncertain economy. I talked on the phone with clients all day. While on the phone, I was watching stocks and reading the latest news. If I wasn't transacting business, I was meeting prospects and existing clients. At that time, I was responsible for managing over $120 million in assets.

Most of the clients in the partnership book of business were not African American and the partnership was not equally balanced. It was (and is) my desire to manage the same amount of money with a majority of minority clients. I realized that with all my education and expertise, I still had difficulty getting through to the very people I wanted so badly to empower. I needed to evaluate the reason for my dilemma and I've come to the following conclusions. To be successful in the financial services business, you must have the ability to produce results quickly, regardless of race. While you may create a business plan that includes solicitation to your fellow sisters and brothers, it takes more time to develop relationships with black clients. Therefore, because the pressure is on, any rational individual with a desire to remain in the business must seriously consider moving on. I know many colleagues who have been unsuccessful in their attempts. Sadly, I experienced a time when I could speak with a new prospect and, based on my credentials, the prospect could determine almost instantly if they were going to transfer their accounts to me. However, when dealing with minority prospects, it would take me almost three times as long to convert a new account. Most often, it would take longer to transfer less. I attribute this hesitation to lack of knowledge. There aren't enough minority experts in the field of finance and historically we have not had exposure to the financial world. Therefore, how can one respect the qualifications of an expert? Furthermore, we have leadership without experience teaching us how to become financially free.

But we are a target. During the last decade, we have experienced a flood of minority advisors being hired at boutique firms, mutual fund companies, and small investment banks because someone realized there is wealth in our communities.

What was holding me back from working with people of my culture? Originally I felt it was their lack of financial knowledge but after having success, I realized that most people just don't know how to get started, and, yes, what to do and why. That is why I originally felt the need to write this book. I believe this book will serve as a basic fundamental tool that will allow people to read experiences, ideas and various client relationships that will help evaluate their own lives. I decided to revise the book because I don't want you the reader to just *think* about your very own situations. I want you to begin *changing* them. Therefore, if the first message of how to get started wasn't clear, this book will serve as a step-by-step manual. Five years later, I'm more sensitive to even the emotional relationships our culture has with finances and I believe we can overcome the challenges together.

Entertainers and athletes are in the public eye and live their lives as an open book. We fantasize about their experiences and identify with their story even though it doesn't represent our life. Unfortunately, often we look to entertainers or sports professionals for overall advice. But should we try to model our lifestyles and way of living by the lives of these entertainers? Or would typical stories that occur in the average family be more effective and meaningful to us?

Seeing all too clearly the issues at hand, it was time for me to begin the work God wanted me to do. I began to write one week after my thirtieth birthday. Sitting at my computer at home, I was very focused and committed to outlining new goals and objectives for myself. The book was coming along and I was dedicated to writing at least two times a week. I was relying on a disk to store my data and the information was saved in my computer at the office. After losing the data, which I will elaborate on later, I became very frustrated and I decided that a book was not in the cards for me.

In January of the following year, I was awakened early one Saturday morning about 5:30 a.m. Since I usually get up early every morning for either work or church, I was not happy about this on my only day of rest. Nevertheless, the Spirit of the Lord led me downstairs to my computer. Quite honestly, I had not even thought about the book. I didn't think about writing or anything else for the previous three and a half months until I began to read what I had written almost one year earlier. I was amazed. The writings stated my desires and the calling I felt that God had placed on my life. I sat there very early that Saturday morning and wrote my thoughts and my feelings. All of that ultimately led to this moment. So sit back, relax, as I share my story.

THE AWAKENING

At the age of six, I would envision what my life would be like at the age of thirty. To a little girl, thirty is old. I had mapped out my entire life because I believed if I could achieve certain goals, I could be productive to society, and live the life I imagined. When I became an adult, I realized thirty is not old so I used that birthday as a measuring post to evaluate my life.

It is amazing that children do not comprehend the words "no," "can't," and "impossible" when they allow their imaginations to wander freely. Confident that they can achieve almost anything, kids tend to be very detail-oriented and specific about what life will look like when they grow up. Many of my childhood goals may sound familiar to most women. I want to be married with two children, a boy and a girl. "I want the boy to be older than the girl so he can take care of his little sister." While playing house, my imagination would roam down many avenues of what life would be like when I got older. I dreamed of having a Cape Cod house with a white picket fence. I wanted to be the best trial attorney on the east coast and well on my way to being appointed the first

African American Supreme Court Judge. I didn't even know about Thurgood Marshall. So imagine my disappointment when I thought Clarence Thomas beat me to the punch. At least I still had a chance to be the first Black Vice President (I thought).

At the age of thirty, I realized how truly blessed I am to be married to my perfect mate and the mother of two beautiful children, Jesse and Emani. And yes, my son is older than his sister by five years. I have a beautiful house in a nice, quiet neighborhood. The one goal I did not accomplish was being an attorney. Life has its twists and turns, but I managed to find a career I loved so much it overrode my political aspirations and desires. I became a certified financial planner and financial advisor with a relationship with the entertainment industry. I am a small business owner. I have had the privilege of hosting both a television show and radio broadcast. It is my commitment to utilize those channels to educate and empower people spiritually, mentally, and financially. Every time a viewer or listener shares their life story with me, I feel honored. What is most rewarding is when they reference something I had said.

As a financial planner, I develop a relationship with my clients as that of an extended family member and valuable friend. I fully understand the intimacy of exposing finances with another individual. With that knowledge, I can appreciate being included in family outings. I do laugh when family members express their amazement at the fact that the host has a planner or they've seen me on television. But something powerful often happens—people begin to realize that they can explore a relationship with an advisor and they can begin to put their financial affairs in order. Personally, I appreciate knowing who my client's attorneys and accountants are. I like knowing who they are using when they purchase a house. Why? Because they call me to ask for a recommendation or speak with the person they selected. I am still overwhelmed, even to this day, when I see the look on someone's face when they've realized their dream to purchase a house or they've accumulated enough money to cover their children's college needs or they can start the business they always dreamed of or they can retire five years earlier than planned if they desire.

All of this is based on a plan we devised together and reviewed periodically. Most of them are comforted with the possibility of achieving those goals. And those same family members and friends begin to look at my client's differently. It is the look that says, "How can he/she afford an advisor? Where do they stand financially?" And most important, "Why don't I have advisor? I need to get myself together."

Even with all of that, I always considered my vocation a valuable necessity for the client. It was very rewarding, but a job nonetheless. I can go even further and say it was my career. I loved what I did for a living. But the one thing I never realized was how important it was to have a plan prior to going through an experience where you would need a plan.

MEASURING POSTS

When you were a child, what did you dream about?

What would it take for you to achieve your goals?

Do you have a plan?

A LIFE
CHANGING EVENT

On the morning of September 11th, I went to work bright and early. I worked on the 73rd floor in the World Trade Center building two. It was primary election day in New York City. It was a beautiful day, a clear blue sky, people hustling, scrambling off to work.

Most people knew I was in my office because I was a workaholic. The state of the economy in 2001 and the fact that I was at a new firm deemed I work an average of seventy hours each week. I'd just celebrated my one year anniversary with my new job the month before. Between the market being down and my team still trying to adjust to the new surroundings, it was amazing that any of us had a chance to go home at night to rest. We practically lived at the office transferring assets from one company to the next. This was very time consuming. In order to make sure each client is well taken care of, as a financial planner, clients must have every incentive they previously had at the old firm. Those details often take a year to eighteen months to accomplish.

Quite frankly, because of the time restrictions, and my personal desire to work independently, I made a very difficult decision to separate from the team and begin working on my own. This was always my intention. When we decided to transfer firms, I indicated that I would help transition our client base which generally takes three to six months. Afterwards, I would begin to concentrate on developing my own book of business while still supporting the team. After the first year, I would slowly transition out of the team. After working together for eight years, my associate and I wanted the clients to get used to the idea that I would no longer be around.

However, things did not work out quite the way I intended. Because of the condition of the market, I never had the opportunity to fully concentrate on my own business. Therefore, I made an executive decision that no time would be the best time. At that point, I experienced major relief. At the end of 2001, it was my plan to be on my own, walking into my own destiny and fulfilling the plan of action God desired for me. So there wasn't any question about my whereabouts on the morning of September 11th.

As you are now aware, tragedy stuck that morning when we were attacked by spineless terrorists. I had come into my office and laid my briefcase down. I was preparing to speak to one of the interns from the team because some changes were about to take place in the office. Originally, I was scheduled to leave my partnership in December of the same year; however, after serious contemplation and several meetings with management, a mutual decision was made to terminate the partnership that I was in for the last eight years immediately, effective September 15th.

So, I came out of my office and stopped at the desk to speak with an assistant. That's when Tower One was hit. We could feel the initial impact of the plane in Tower Two. The building began to vibrate and the lights flickered off and on. There was a lot of movement. I think this may have lasted a full thirty seconds but it felt like two or three minutes. I couldn't see anything based on where my office was located, so I did not panic immediately.

As a matter of fact, my two assistants wanted to leave. But at the time, I didn't think it was necessary. As an advisor, my thinking was about making money and I needed to be at my desk to do that. If a financial advisor is not at his/her desk evaluating or researching a stock, speaking to a client, or placing orders, that advisor would be out attracting new clients. Our ultimate objective was to make money for our clients. Not to mention properly servicing our clients greatly increases our potential for financial freedom.

I walked across the hall to my partner's office and looked out the window. What I saw was burning papers twirling in the wind. It reminded me of a ticker tape parade to celebrate when the New York Yankees won the World Series. As I looked out the window in disbelief, the Spirit of the Lord spoke, telling me to leave. I did not hesitate. Moving quickly, I went into my office, grabbed my briefcase, and told my assistants, "Let's go!" They eagerly followed having made the same suggestion not even one minute earlier.

On our way to the staircase on the 73rd floor, we

passed the receptionist desk. I shared what God had told me and she grabbed her purse and left with us. (Let this be a message to you. Sometimes you don't need to hear directly from God for the message to apply to you.) Apparently we were some of the first ones to leave the floor. I later learned that several male associates had made sure almost everyone left the floor.

Many of my colleagues caught the elevator to the 44th floor and then walked down. A number of us took the staircase. Announcements were being made over the public announcement system, *"Building Two is secure, Building Two is secure. You can go back to your office. Building Two is secure. You are safe. You can choose to leave the building, but I assure you Building Two is secure."* This announcement was made over and over again. As a matter of fact, I found comfort in the announcement.

Meanwhile, as we were walking down the steps, word began to spread through the stairway that Building One had been hit by an airplane. I thought it was an accident. Perhaps a small CNN plane had lost control and hit the Tower, nothing major …just a small accident.

Someone opened the door to the 53rd floor stairway and I decided to take the elevator down to the 44th floor and ride back up to my office. At that point, somehow my assistants and I were temporarily separated. We are taught as children that whenever an emergency occurs, do not get on an elevator …use the stairs. Getting on the elevator was probably one of the stupidest decisions I have ever made in my life. But I took the elevator from the 53rd floor to the 44th floor.

Let me explain something about the 44th floor. If you've ever been in the World Trade Center, then you know that the 44th floor is where you can take different elevators to your designated floor. So for me to get back to the 73rd floor, I had to go through the 44th floor. When I got there, I glanced at the TV monitors confirming the story I heard on the staircase regarding the plane. What was not yet confirmed was that it was a CNN plane and that it was not an accident. I reconnected with my assistants and walked over to the elevators. I hesitated. I thank God because the hesitation saved my life.

When the elevator came, once again, I *felt* the Spirit of the Lord telling me to wait. I did not get on the elevator. That's when Tower Two was hit—the building that I was in—the building that was secure. The plane went right through the floors that I was returning to. Immediately, I knew we were being attacked. Elevator chutes popped, causing explosions and fireballs to shoot out. People died on the elevators that I had just exited. People standing outside of the elevator doors were severely burned. I was standing in front of an elevator that did not open. The first thing I did was drop to my knees and pray. I said, "Father, please forgive me." If I did not survive, if I did not make it out of that building, I would be in heaven today without a shadow of doubt. After that, I began to pray, "God, cover me, God, cover the people I'm with. Let us get out of here safely."

My assistant asked me later that day how I had the mind, attitude, and the strength to pray at that precise moment. I told her that I didn't have a choice. What else would I do? If we were to have any chance of surviving, it would have to be God's will. I had to let my specific requests be made known unto the Lord. I wanted to survive.

At the same time, bodies were flying because of the impact of the plane. The building was shaking, glass shattered everywhere, and smoke began to infiltrate the 44th floor. After what seemed like fifty years, but was probably closer to four or five minutes, a dead calm began to gulf the air. The chaos just died down, almost instantly. I did not stick around. The Lord spoke to me for the third time, instructing me to walk to a stairway that I did not even know had existed.

It's funny how we can work in an environment and not commit our surroundings to our memories. I never realized how important it is to observe your exit points everywhere you go. I began to walk down the stairway and there was an eerie calm. Usually, when faced with a potentially dangerous situation, there is chaos and confusion. But on that day, September 11th, that did not happen. As a matter of fact, I thought it was very ironic that the stairway was not crowded. There were floors where it was almost empty. As I was walking down, there was no smoke and the area was well lit. On the 44th floor, it was apparent something serious had occurred. You could really see the effects of the tragedy. On the stairs, there was no activity. If I had not been in the building, I would have imagined the whole situation. I began to question the severity of the incident. I was convincing myself that it was not as significant as our being attacked although I knew in my spirit that being attacked is what truly happened.

We connected with a young lady on the staircase who was asthmatic. Walking down the stairs was beginning to seriously affect her breathing. It was decided that we were all going to get out of the building together. I said to her, "We're not going to leave you. So if you need to stay here, I'll stand with you. I know I'm getting out of the building safely, but I prefer not to stop. So if you must have an attack, I'd appreciate it if you could wait until we got to Broadway." Needless to say, she did get out of the building with us.

Although I felt comfort on the stairway, I still knew we were under attack and while walking down the stairs, the news that the Pentagon had been hit and another plane crashed in Pennsylvania spread and that news laid heavy on my heart. As far as I was concerned, another plane could be on the way. I knew we were still in trouble.

I did not realize the devastation that had occurred until I hit the mezzanine. If you know anything about the World Trade Center, it was known for its glass panes. The panes stemmed from the ground to the ceiling. The revolving doors were made of glass; glass was everywhere. The mezzanine was once a beautiful place to visit and just gaze outside. Many pictures have been taken on the mezzanine of the World Trade Center. When I hit the mezzanine, my first thought was "*Freedom!*" Those glass doors represented an escape for me. Go through the revolving doors and run! I would have been running for my dear life. I could get out of a situation that could be potentially dangerous, hazardous to my health. It might kill me.

The greatest fear that I had the entire day came at that point. There were firemen and police officers telling me that I could not exit out of those doors—the very doors that led to freedom for me. They were holding me captive.

Little did I know, debris was falling everywhere and it

was to my advantage not to go that route. I thank God for the professionals. The policemen and firemen represented true heroism on September 11th. But the hardest thing that I had to do on that day was to walk further into the World Trade Center. I had to go downstairs to the floor where all of the stores were. I walked passed the Diamond Hut, Strawberries, the N&R trains, the Watch Store, The Disney Store, Nine West; all of the stores that I visited almost weekly. Every so often, medics and authorities would pass the crowd of people, attempting to get out of the building with an injured man or woman. I saw people bleeding profusely, limbs cut off, shocked people experiencing asthma attacks, people who probably never had heart conditions experiencing pains in the chest. I saw everything you would not wish on your worst enemy. Ironically, in hindsight, the vision of the movie *Dead Man Walking* can effectively describe how I felt. The point when the convict who was about to be executed had to walk the long corridor to his death. It was at that moment I felt most vulnerable. I was full of despair, lacking hope because I knew that life as we were accustomed, would never be the same. If I ever thought death was knocking on my door, it was while I was walking down that long, long corridor. But as quickly as that thought came, I rebuked it. I was going to get out of that building.

I later heard that a friend said while comforting one of my sisters before they heard from me, "Nicole is going to get out of the building even if she has to shimmy down the wall. Now you know your sister." Her comment actually provided comic relief in the midst of a tough situation.

After going up the escalator, I was finally out of the building. I exited for the last time, Building 5, right next to the infamous Krispy Kreme Doughnut Shop. I did not turn around. I just kept walking. I walked and thanked God but I did not look back. God had given Lot and his wife identical instructions. *If you turn around, you will surely die.*

When I reached Broadway, I finally turned around. I saw an airplane sitting in the building that I had just come out of. It seemed unreal ...like a picture. There I was standing on Broadway Avenue looking at the World Trade Center with an airplane in it. I have no recollection of what Building One looked like or what had happened to the first plane. What I do remember is that the sky was clear, a perfect blue with little or no clouds in sight. An airplane's wings were hanging out the building. The flames were a precise, burnt orange, and clouds of smoke swirled perfectly in the air. The picture would have been worthy of art had the experience not been a reality. I never expected to see bodies falling out the sky and people attempting to jump from a skyscraper. Tears began to stream down my face. I had not cried the entire time beforehand. I was trying to be strong for my assistants who were traumatized at that moment. But that was the last straw. I believe everyone cried at one point or another. I still have visions and dreams to this day. I have seen things I will never forget, certain things that will haunt me or at least sober me for the rest of my life. There are recollections that hinder me from sleeping more often than I'd care to remember. But I'm mindful that God desired to save me. It was at that moment I began to realize that I was not far enough away from the

World Trade Center. Call it instinct; call it God watching over me. All I knew was that we needed to move, and we needed to move quickly.

Mind you, we never attempted to communicate with our loved ones to let them know we were still alive. So while on Broadway, we tried to make phone calls. I managed to get through to my sister's job in New York City, but she did not go to work on that day. She was in New Jersey enrolling my niece into a new school. So my family had to wait hours before hearing from me. I decided to walk over to Battery Park City.

At that moment, I thought about my associate. She had decided to vote before coming to work. Therefore, based on her anticipated time of arrival in the office, I half expected her to be near, or even in the building. Either way, I always had complete access to her home so at least I would be able to use the phone to try and reach my family.

Four of us began to walk, proceeding down the block toward Fulton Street. We moved on to Wall Street and then to Battery Park. We circled around the FDR Drive. But before we crossed the street to continue on our way to Battery Park City, we stood near the overpass just gazing up at the sky. From that vantage point we were able to see things we should have never looked for. You could see the tail of the plane hanging out. So instantly I knew that it was where the plane initially hit. I felt so close. I could actually see people, people that I knew were going to die that day because it was impossible for them to exit the building.

When we finally arrived at Battery Park City on Rector Street, we found my associate alive and very happy to see us. The first thing we did was hug and cry together. The five of us stood praying, crying, meditating and thanking God. As soon as we got to her home, Building Two, the building I used to work in, the building I had just come out of, the building where I must have left at least seven pairs of shoes, collapsed. It just fell.

I never, ever, even in my wildest dreams, imagined those buildings could and would be destroyed. But I was safe, safe from the bricks, safe from the falling debris, the broken glass, everything. The only thing that traveled my way was the dust particles. Rector Street was a blanket of dust. Dust was in the air, traveling in the windows, into people's houses and into my lungs. When the building fell, it became as dark as a pitch-black sky in the heart of the country. The smoke was so thick the sky that once was blue, turned midnight for at least thirty minutes. I don't know the actual time between Building Two and Building One falling, but I do know that the skies had just begun to clear from the collapse of the Building Two when Building One put us back into the pitch-dark nighttime atmosphere. My heart fell with the fall of the two buildings. A piece of my soul died on that day.

We were unsuccessful in communicating with our families. Shortly after the second tower collapsed, the electricity failed in the building we were in. No lights, no TV, no radio—nothing. The only thing that was still working was the telephone. And to this very day, I'm still not certain how that was even possible. Even my associate's laptop gave way after a while. When we first arrived at the house, it was still up and running. We began to email family and friends. That was nothing but the grace of God.

I finally had a chance to speak with my family a little after 12:00 noon. The first person I spoke with was my mom. I could not reach my husband and I knew he was worried sick about me. My husband, Jesse, was home getting ready for work. He is a TV producer and director who often does freelance work with outside cable companies. After getting dressed, he got into the car and began to drive. He turned on the radio and heard the personality tell everyone to stay calm, don't panic. Instantly, he thought another artist had passed away. As he was driving, the news that one of the Twin Towers had been hit smacked him in the face making him lose his breath. He didn't even make it off the block.

Immediately, he drove the car in reverse down the block back to the house. Ironically, as he got out of the car, he looked across the street and noticed several middle-eastern men cutting down a tree in one of the neighbor's yards. We had never seen these men before and I cannot recall ever seeing them at anytime thereafter.

Jesse walked into the house leaving the front door wide open. A neighbor came to the house to make sure the he was holding up well. He was sitting in front of the television attempting to convince himself that I was in the tower that had not been hit. That was until the second building was hit. Then he was trying to convince himself that I was in the first building. Why? Because based on where the buildings were hit, I still had a chance to survive had I been in building one. By that time, several neighbors had gathered at my house. They were all watching TV in my living room hoping for the best when Tower Two collapsed. Jesse sat in utter disbelief still hoping and praying that I was still alive. But shortly after Tower Two fell, Tower One came down too. That was it. He thought I was dead. Any chance of my being alive was crushed along with the buildings. He said he began to think: what did I wear to work that day, what did I smell like, did he tell me that he loved me.

He said he forgot that he had children and had it not been for the neighbors reminding him about the children, he would not have remembered them. He did go to the school to pick up our son, Jesse, who had overheard the teachers talking about the Towers collapsing. So by the time my husband went to the school, my son was dealing with the thought that his mother was dead. When he saw his dad coming into the school building, he felt that was a confirmation of his greatest fear. My husband made the decision to let five-year-old Emani stay in school since she did not know what was going on. It was the best thing he could have done. She did not have to suffer with the thought of her mommy not coming home ever again. It was bad enough for Lil' Jesse to deal with that trauma.

Interestingly enough, he deals with it even today. If I'm leaving the house, he questions me as if he is my dad. He wants to know where I'm going, who I'm going to be with and what time will I get back. I tell him that I'm the mom and he is still the child. I'll be okay. Fortunately, my husband and my son heard from me by about 1:00 in the afternoon. They did not have to wait twenty-four to forty-eight hours like some of the horror stories of the other survivors.

Shortly after we were all able to reach our loved ones, early in the afternoon, security in Battery Park City began to cry loudly on each floor. They were knocking

on everyone's door. The building was being evacuated.
Our experience was hardly over. As we made our way
from the second floor to outside, relying on our hands
to feel the walls and using flashlights in the darkness, I
began to wonder where I was going. How was I going to
get home?

I walked out of Battery Park City and immediately I
knew my true purpose in life. Why? Security was direct-
ing all of the residents to the water to get on boats to
either Jersey City or Staten Island. Yes, boats. They
had both cargo and freight boats available for evacua-
tion. Understand …there were provisions in place to
take the wealthy to safety. I realized at that moment the
wealthy had plans in place to provide for unforeseen circumstances, unforeseen incidents. As a culture, African
Americans don't have a plan and I realized how seriously
we needed to get one.

Now the people in Battery Park City do not look like
you and me. I have friends, associates, and colleagues
who got home after midnight. Many of them had to wait
until the next day. I was fortunate enough to get home
by 4:00 in the afternoon because first and foremost,
I had favor with God and favor ain't fair! I was at the
right place at the right time, benefiting from the provision the wealthy set up for themselves. I was not there by
accident. I began to think, as I got on a large, cargo boat,
that I was safe. Finally, that part of my life, that tragedy
was almost over. But no, that would have been too easy.
I truly believe God has a sense of humor, even when I
know certain things are not funny.

While on a boat going toward Jersey City, New Jersey,
which was my hometown, we received word that the boat

we were on was too large to dock at the port. So we had to change boats in the middle of the water. So now I have a vision of surviving the Word Trade Center attack only to fall off of the boat while transferring onto another and not surviving. I began to laugh hysterically with tears falling down my face. I had lost control and could not understand why this was happening to me. No shoes, covered with dust, clothes torn—broken. But again, I had survived. I got down to Jersey City and looked immediately for ways to go home. My assistants, my associate and I stayed together until this point and once in Jersey City, we parted ways. My associate who lived in Battery Park City went home with me to meet up with a friend. I lived approximately forty-five minutes away and I didn't want to go to my momma's house or my in-laws house. I wanted to go home to my house with my family. I managed to meet my mother-in-law because God granted her favor. Jersey City was completely shut down but the police officers allowed her to break through the barriers to pick me up. Traffic was being directed away from downtown but she was given permission to drive in that direction.

Ironically, I have a friend who received a phone call from her sister because she spotted me after I got off the boat. My friend Denise shared that her sister said I was alive, I was okay but I looked a mess. And I really did. No jacket or shoes, covered with dust from head to toe with gray hair. Denise knew I was in the building. The instant she heard about the Tower getting hit, she called everyone in my church family to begin a prayer vigil. She also gathered up some clothes, food, shoes and other essentials and dragged her daughter,

Bianca, downtown. I'm sure Bianca had no idea what was going on but they managed to convince authorities that I was in need. They let Denise go all the way to Exchange Place and down by the harbor. I never saw her that day because not only did my phone not work, I put all of my energy into getting home.

Finally, I arrived home around 4:00 p.m. and I completely embraced my family. Once my associate was gone, I began to watch television. I sat in my living room for six or seven days watching the death toll continue to rise. I watched what happened in Pennsylvania, in Washington, and in New York, over and over again. I did not leave my seat, I didn't sleep. During that time, I left my house to accomplish two tasks—to go to the hospital because I could not breathe and to my mother's house so she could be firmly convinced that I was alive and in the flesh. I couldn't even stay in the hospital because I didn't feel safe. I really thought the hospital could be attacked. So against the doctor's advice, I check out. What did I do? I got back on my couch and continued to torture myself. The death toll continued to rise and I just kept thanking God over and over again. Why not me, Lord? Why was I spared? Thank you, Lord! Thank you, Lord! I would unexpectedly fall to my knees to pray scaring my husband in the process.

I thank God for Jesse because after hearing my entire ordeal, he protected me from reliving the story over and over again. He carried the burden, spoke to everyone who voiced concern and sheltered me while I was in a vulnerable state. Protecting my privacy and honoring my wishes, he would not allow me to speak to anyone. Now that I think about it, he went through a major trauma as well. He forgot about his needs; bearing the pain and agony he went through thinking I was dead. I am honored to be in a relationship with such an awesome man.

As some point, on the forth or the fifth day, I began to think. What if? What would have happened if I had not survived? What if I were permanently disabled? Many people lost arms, legs, and internal organs. Others were severely burned.

Point of fact, you didn't have to experience the tragedy of the World Trade Center to experience disability. You are more likely to face some form of disability than premature death. If you're injured and you can't work, can you maintain your standard of living or would your lifestyle change dramatically? I began to think about all of the people who lost their jobs. What if? Where would my family be? What was the state of my household? Did I have a plan in place? I began to evaluate my situation. As a result of my personal testimony I generally ask my clients the very same questions I had asked myself.

MEASURING POSTS

Name an experience in your life that made
you reflect on the true purpose of life.

If you could change your future,
where would you begin?

What is stopping you? Time? Money? Fear?

DO YOU HAVE
A PLAN?

At that point of my life being a financial planner took on an entirely different meaning, having lived through an ordeal myself. Being a mother of two young children, married and blessed with a home in a nice community made me realize how vulnerable I could possibly be. We are probably classified as a middle class income household. My home was not completely paid yet. My husband and I largely rely on each other's income to maintain our standard of living.

Jesse and I have desires and dreams for each of our children. If they choose to go to Harvard, we want to be able to make that dream come true. If I had not survived, would my husband have to worry about how the bills were going to be paid the following month? Better yet, could he lose the house because he can no longer afford to meet the monthly mortgage payments? Would my family have to suffer emotionally with losing a wife and mother and simultaneously be subject to moving back to the very same neighborhood we worked so hard to get out of. Did I have insurance in place? Did I have emergency cash set aside?

After contemplating the things most important to me, I came to the conclusion that working seventy hours a week was no longer acceptable to me. I wanted to be around to see my children grow up. Financially, that is not a decision one can make overnight. I decided to figure out, even if I could not afford it at that precise moment, how would I change my plans to open that opportunity in the near future? I realized the importance of putting a plan of action in place prior to needing one. That's where many of us end up in a difficult position.

Before beginning the process of implementing a plan, you have the chance to evaluate your relationship with your significant partner, your children, your grandchildren. What type of impact do you desire to have in their lives? You can maintain a certain lifestyle when you're alive, when you are capable of working, but what about when you can't work. I thank God I had a financial plan that included provisions for death, disability, and loss of income. When developing a plan, you must evaluate what is truly important to you and begin to work toward those goals.

Through that evaluation process, you can make the decision whether or not you need a new job, additional schooling, or should you just step out on faith and start that business you have been dreaming about for years. Are you one of those people who keeps a detailed plan of how to carry out your dreams in a notebook that goes everywhere you go? Every time you talk to your friends, are you telling them something new about how you would make your dreams come true? When is the time to act on those plans?

Through my entire ordeal, the one thing my husband said was he never thought about our financial state, God forbid, had I not survived. He was assured that we had a plan in place. That has always been the security I would want should I ever have to face a life-threatening situation again. I relied upon our plan also as I made the decision not to return to work immediately after the tragedy. There were several reasons for my decision.

First, my firm had relocated our office to the Madison Square Garden. The first day that everyone went into the office, there was a bomb scare at the Garden. My colleagues had to walk down thirty-four flights of stairs. Any thoughts I may have had about going there to work were quickly erased. I figured I was an educated woman with an excellent work track record. If my company could not find a place for me in New Jersey, then I would be forced to consider other options.

Secondly, from a business perspective, since I had to start from scratch again, it would benefit me to start in a place I was familiar with and around people who knew something about me. Because my husband and I owned a television production company that was known for creating original programming, I've had the opportunity to host a television show for several years. That platform assisted me in creating relationships with various community leaders, which ultimately led my company to get involved locally through a community association. Being active in the community and being on television everyday worked to my advantage.

At any rate, for the first time since giving birth to my

son, my paycheck would be similar to the income I was making in high school. It was like starting all over but would the sacrifices be worth it?

In the times we now live in, I am not the only one that sees the need to determine what sacrifices we might and should make to benefit our loved ones in the future. The question for many is where do you start?

MEASURING POSTS

What do you consider a priority in your
life-Family, money, social status?

Are you satisfied with your accomplishments to date?

What steps can you make to improve
your circumstances?

PREPARING YOUR FAMILY FOR EMERGENCIES

Having money set aside for emergencies would probably be the most immediate need for many families today. If I didn't have such a plan in place I wouldn't have had the peace of mind to pursue my deepest endeavors. Upon my decision to leave work, emergency cash money subsidized my family income replacing what I originally contributed to the household. But, it was not all easy.

Many days I would question my husband to make sure I had the support I needed to redevelop a new business in order to educate my community and develop a new clientele. I also decided to take a hiatus from the family television business as well. I knew, based on my business plan, building a new clientele would be difficult and time consuming. I didn't want to be an unnecessary financial burden to him. I was already nervous about stepping out on faith, but my husband was very supportive. He could have told me to get a new job. Instead of building a business, I could have been waiting tables.

Besides having an emergency plan in place, it was critical to have a support system during the transition. My husband's support gave me the opportunity to develop my business on a firm, solid foundation. It could be built to most effectively benefit my clients. Now I was in a position to get started evaluating the needs of the people who desired to gain control of their finances. Not everyone has the encouragement and/or the support I had to develop financial strategies and plans for the future. I want to become your support system.

Again from my experience, I was able to assess the circumstances and needs of the people I wanted to serve. I understood I would need to make it mandatory for my clients to complete a financial plan before seriously discussing investment strategies. This is the best way to see what needs and issues exist. There are exceptions to every rule. Not all clients see the need to do this, especially those primarily interested in seeking only investment strategies. Still, I inform them about the importance of having a plan and strongly suggest they consider putting one in place if they don't already have on. In addition, for personal reasons, I choose not to work with individuals who have their own agenda. The reason? You entertain the thought of working with someone because you assume they should know more than you. Therefore, if you believe your plan is the better plan, then you don't need me. It is extremely dangerous to focus on wealth accumulation without any concentration on possible scenarios that can hinder you from achieving your financial goals.

Most of us see the importance of maintaining a plan for emergencies but few of us see the urgency of setting the plan up immediately. Some think it sounds good and it's something they will eventually get around to. But I want to take you back to my September 11th experience. The wealthy had provisions that not only assisted them in getting to safety, but many of them were capable of taking up residence in another city, another state.

As we reflect on the natural disaster called Hurricane Katrina, I believe many of us were taken aback at the lack of financial and emotional support that was provided by the government. People were advised to get out of the state of Louisiana. For residents without the financial resources or the ability to move quickly, minimal provisions were made. Most of the individuals in dire need of assistance were African American citizens. Several challenges were faced. First, many people did not have money because it was the end of the month and perhaps just shy of pay day or the day that government assistance would be made available. Second, after the tragedy, for the individuals with some resources, moving to another city or state was equally overwhelming because everything they owned was lost or destroyed. They had to start all over. The correlation between September 11th and Hurricane Katrina is that the wealthy utilized their resources to evacuate the premises. These are two totally different experiences with a common provision. Your emergency could come next week. The real possibility of becoming unemployed will always exist. Natural disasters will always occur. Disability will always hit close to home. Just in case you don't get the picture. We've faced extreme weather patterns, major unexpected plane collisions such as Flight 587 in Queens, New York, and the earthquake in Hawaii, etc.

While the state of the economy is currently gaining strength from year to year—especially since the peak in the market in March of 2000 and the war in Iraq and Afghanistan—many corporations are forced to undergo major layoffs to reduce company expenses. This trend occurred prior to September 11th. We all know someone who has been laid off, offered an early retirement package or a severance package.

For African Americans in particular, a severance package may appear to be the world's greatest gift. Very often the package is determined by the years of service to the company. But not so fast ...immediately Uncle Sam is entitled to his share. So maybe you will receive two thirds of what you originally anticipated. Now do you create a budget with the thought in mind that jobs are scarce and you might need to analyze your financial future? Or do you run and buy that car you have been dreaming about, adding to your monthly household expenses? What about the new living room set, or the washing machine? I got it. You've been working since you graduated high school and you need a vacation. Finally you have the resources to go on your dream vacation. Just a thought, but you might need that money in a few months when you're still unemployed.

If we budget ourselves accordingly, this scenario could apply to you. It's so amazing how we can save $100 per month for a whole year toward a vacation but we can't save $100 a month for emergencies. Imagine if you received that same severance package and you had three months of your monthly expenses set aside. In addition you will file for unemployment. That plan just gave you six months to look for a new employer. How? Rather than running out and spending the money as soon as you got it, by setting aside the money to pay your bills your existing lifestyle would not be dramatically affected.

How many times have you had extra money but chose not to think ahead about future bills and you paid the price later? Suffering a disability or loss of a job can be devastating when you don't have an emergency plan in place for such unexpected situations. Some people have even lost their homes to foreclosure because of the lack of proper planning and saving money. Do you want to be in a position like that?

When I make statements like that, I always hear people say, "I can't afford to save money, it's just not possible." People even say what I promote is unrealistic in urban communities. Unfortunately, the reality is that most Americans are living from paycheck to paycheck. Or they are approximately two months away from eviction.

But let's look at how we spend money. I find it amazing that women can't set aside money for emergencies but they don't miss a hair appointment. The cheapest hairstyle is a wash and set (or doobie). An average doobie costs at least $30.00. That must be maintained weekly creating a monthly bill of $120.00. We get our nails done twice a month and if we throw in a pedicure, we just spent another $50.00. A design and tip refills add another $30.00 per month. We work hard all week and need a break so girl's night out once a month is mandatory. I'll give you that you're getting into the party for free. But even the best looking ladies must pay for the first drink so she doesn't give off that she is waiting for a man to pay for her enjoyment. The outfit you purchased cost approximately $65 and you bought that on sale.

For all of you that attend church on Sunday morning, there are certain churches that a new outfit each month is a must. Now church is a totally different expense. Why? You've got to look good for God. An entire ensemble just might run you approximately $100. And if you throw in the hat, you've just spent another $30.

Now I'm not just picking on the women because men have their devices as well. Some men spend so much money on maintenance of their automobiles. A bottle of Armor All, Fresh Scent, and Turtle Wax totals about $15. The instant you get a spot on your white on white Air Force Ones, it's time for a new pair because cleaning them is not an option. That costs $150 given the size of your foot. Now the clubs the ladies get into for free cost you $20. Men generally hit the clubs twice a month totaling $40. Buying drinks as soon as you get in will cost you, especially if it's a classy joint. You can spend almost $150 before you even blink. That's because you require Hennessy or other top shelf liquor. Your clothes are so expensive and unfortunately, you don't have any stores like the ladies' $10 spot. Each outfit runs you at least $150 if you want to attract wifey. If not, $100 will do if you don't want to be the laughing stock of the party. Men must look like they're rolling in dough. But (just to drive the point home) the average man is driving around in a car that he can't really afford. If your car note is over

$500 and you are living in subsidized housing with your girl, that right there needs to be analyzed.

Finally, for everyone that works everyday and says you can't save, answer this question: Do you bring your lunch to work? If the answer is no, you're probably spending at least $7 for lunch. Normally you pick up coffee and a bagel for $2 and if you're anything like me, at about 3:00 each afternoon, you crave for a soda and a snack running you an additional $2. If you total that up, that's about $11 per day give or take a dollar or two. By the end of the week you spent $55 and each month that totals $220.

Okay, I'm going to get banned out of church for this one, but the Bible says bring your tithes and offering to the storehouse that there might be meat in God's house Malachi 3:10. God challenges us to prove Him that He would pour out a blessing that we would not have room enough to receive. Many people don't tithe. They just don't trust that part of God's Word. It is precisely at this point we decide that God knows our heart and our circumstances. But even with that, when there is a prayer line for a blessing if you bring $100, $50, and $20, we are quick to seek out the swift blessings that are often contrary to the Word of God. Many of us put that money in the church, not adhering to what is required and will risk our lights being shut off, or our doors being locked. There aren't any quick fix methods and regardless of how many conferences you attend with wealthy, nationally acclaimed pastors and you keep giving the sacrificial offerings to get out of debt, it is for nothing if you don't pay your tithes and offering. But just not to lose focus on my point, the extra $100 to $200 you give to the church for all of the extra-curricular activities can be earmarked for your savings. After all, I promise you that the pastor's mortgage gets paid every month.

Now these examples don't apply to everyone, just the people who say they can't save. Evaluate the choices you make. I do have clients who *really* can't afford to save money. But even they can save for retirement. We must remember each of us will encounter a situation where the need for emergency cash will arise.

For example, while I was still rebuilding my business, my husband, my daughter and I were in a car accident, which totaled my car. Now, living in the suburbs means you must have transportation. We needed to buy another vehicle right away. Emergency cash set aside made that possible.

During the winter, water heaters tend to burst. If that were to happen to you, must you sacrifice the mortgage payment to fix the heater, or to get a new one? Now that's an emergency—that's what the money should be for.

Entertainers and aspiring artists need to be more mindful of having available resources. Why do many entertainers file for bankruptcy? Here's my opinion. I look at the lifestyle of entertainers, particularly music artists. Very often, people get caught up in the glamour of success. Because an artist has a hit record on the charts, people perceive that the entertainer is financially secure. After all, they have attained a level of success. Or have they? With this pressure, the artist feels the burden of maintaining a particular image. If Bentley's are the new wave or Cadillac Escalades, how dare they have a Ford Explorer? If everyone is purchasing million dollar homes, having a condo is not good enough. The clothes you wear must be name brand and the diamonds must be carats.

However, most people at the beginning of their careers cannot even afford these things. They become indebted or obligated to the record company and therefore their money is used to pay off major expenses accumulated at the beginning stages of their careers.

The first thing entertainers should do is put themselves on a budget. Most artists cannot guarantee what their income will be in eighteen months. What is hot today may be tired next month. With a budget in place, the likelihood of losing assets through default is minimized. I recommend entertainers set aside a minimum of six months living expenses. Then there is that much time to make additional money through personal appearances, touring, and endorsement deals. Now, if they should want to purchase a home or a fancy car, they would be in a better position financially to make that decision. Too often artists do not properly manage their money or balance their checkbooks. They just continue to spend. When the financial drought comes, the artist is left feeling the pinch of not having money. Diamond rings on your fingers cannot pay the mortgage bills but a six month emergency stash just might help you out.

A close personal friend has been an artist for over twenty years. This gentleman was a pioneer in the Rap industry at a time when they did it for the love of music, not the almighty dollar. I asked him how he spent the money he earned as an artist because it was nothing compared to what entertainers make today. Many times people will set up systematic withdrawals from their accounts and forget about it. This is exactly what happened with my friend. Without realizing it, he had set aside a small portion of his royalties and income from performances into real estate and a savings account. When the royalty checks stopped coming and the invitations dried up, the property he purchased generated income that allowed him to maintain his standard of living. The investments were yielding dividends and returns, and his emergency money was in tack. Years later, he was mindful of how saving a little each time worked to his advantage.

Another emergency that often occurs are unexpected deaths in the family. Must the entire family depend on one family member who had a plan to handle the financial obligations of a funeral? Or do you wait for the sympathy envelopes filled with financial gifts to start flowing in before you can determine what type of procession you can have? What if the services are out of state? Can you just jump on a plane or rent a car and not worry that hotel accommodations are going to devastate you financially? Or must you phone ahead so you can stay with Aunt Mae? Emergencies!

MEASURING POSTS

Determine your mandatory monthly expenses.

Determine where you are spending unnecessary money each month.

Establish an account where you don't have easy access.

Check on your job to see if you can have multiple direct deposit accounts.

Set aside how long you believe it will take to accumulate your emergency cash.

Determine how much money you can commit to saving each pay period.

Set up a direct deposit into the account earmarked for emergency cash.

BUDGET WORKSHEET

CATEGORY	MONTHLY BUDGET AMOUNT	MONTHLY ACTUAL AMOUNT	DIFFERENCE BETWEEN ACTUAL AND BUDGET
INCOME:			
Wages Paid			
Bonuses			
Interest Income			
Capital Gains Income			
Dividend Income			
Miscellaneous Income			
INCOME SUBTOTAL			
EXPENSES:			
Mortgage or Rent			
TV/Cable			
Telephone			
Cell Phone			
Home Repairs/Maintenance			
Car Payments			
Gasoline/Oil			
Gas for Auto			
AutoRepairs/Maintenance/Fees			
Other Transportation (tolls, bus, subway, etc.)			
Child Care			
College Expenses/Tuition			
Auto Insurance			
Home Owners Renters Insurance			
Computer Expense			
Entertainment/Recreation			
Groceries			
Toiletries, Household Products			
Clothing			

Eating Out			
Gifts/Donations			
Tithes/Offering			
Healthcare (medical/dental/vision, inc. insurance)			
Hobbies			
Interest Expense (mortgage, credit cards, fees)			
Magazines/Newspapers			
Federal Income Tax			
State Income Tax			
Social Security/Medicare Tax			
Personal Property tax			
Pets			
Miscellaneous Expense			
EXPENSES SUBTOTAL			
NET INCOME (INCOME LESS EXPENSES)			

Congratulations! You are on your way to building a firm financial foundation.

OBTAINING LIFE INSURANCE

I mentioned that my husband was not concerned about his financial future if I had not survived because we had insurance plans in place. But let me tell you what happened to us. I always told my husband, "Baby, God forbid something should ever happen to me, call Eileen. All of my important papers are in my office in our file." He remembered that. But when the Towers collapsed, all of my important papers collapsed with them. Now, no one could ever predict that. It made me think.

People usually don't know pertinent information if something were to happen to their mates, particularly women. My husband knew exactly where to go to determine where he stood financially. After the tragedy, he inquired about the details of our insurance policies. What type of insurance plans do we have? How much are they? Who are the carriers? Did I set up settlement options? What did he need to contact the companies? I found these to be very important questions. We all should know the answers. My husband no longer took it for granted that someone else would handle the affairs for him.

But even in my preparing additional information for him, I realized I had set up one of our insurance policies to automatically withdraw the premiums out of our checking account quarterly. About six months after the tragedy, I noticed a payment being withdrawn out of the checking account that looked totally unfamiliar. After inquiring about the withdrawal, I realized I had even more insurance than I had originally thought.

Now, if I'm the planner and I didn't know about the additional insurance without records, how would my husband know what to look for? The obvious lesson for me was to have important documents and information in a place easily accessible to the people who will ultimately need it.

So many of us go without obtaining life insurance thinking there will be time in the future. I spoke with a young lady who was going through the process of applying for life insurance. She was a small business owner and a single parent of two boys and a girl. At the tender age of 28, she experienced three deaths of people close to her in one year alone. That was the primary reason she came to see me.

Being an entrepreneur has its advantages, but one significant disadvantage is that the owner is responsible for everything. Health insurance, life insurance, and retirement plans have to be orchestrated by you. As an owner, you must manage the books. Despite the condition of the economy, the bills must still be paid and if the business is slow, you will do anything to keep the business afloat.

With the young lady, the priority of obtaining life insurance began to take a back seat to the overwhelming bills she faced from day to day. Although I was sympathetic, it was my job to delicately show her how vulnerable her children would be if she were in an accident or suffered from premature death or a disability. Normally delaying the process several months may not become a dire issue if she worked in corporate America. Many companies offer minimal insurance policies and health insurance. But in her situation, her need for insurance was an ultimate priority, especially since premature death was an uncertain possibility and she was a mother of three. What if one of the children suffered a health condition that required medical attention? One break of an arm or a leg would financially cripple her.

While she was thinking about finances I was thinking about the well being of her three children. She loved them dearly and did everything she could to provide an acceptable quality of life. I knew she needed someone to advise her and remind her of her originally stated priorities. She worked hard to create opportunity for her children. She was concentrating so much on the present, she needed me to enlighten her to potential future scenarios that would negatively affect the ones she so desperately loved. I knew she would want them to have significant opportunities even if she was incapable of sharing them for some reason. It is very easy to overlook these things when we are just trying to get by today.

One reason I find many people shy away from insurance is because they don't understand what works best for them. So here is a crash course. There are two types of life insurance; term and permanent. By definition term insurance is insurance that covers the insured (you) for a specified period such as one, five, or ten years. Longer term options are available as well as the option to renew. The premiums are paid throughout the life of the policy but at expiration you are faced with a higher premium as you grow older.

Let's start off with a scenario where term insurance makes sense. It is the least expensive option when considering the financial impact. Therefore if you are on an extremely tight budget, term insurance may be the only insurance you can afford. I like to compare it to auto insurance. Hopefully you will never need it but just in case, it's there. Because you should have a policy outside of your employer, if there are children involved, you definitely need to pick up a term policy at least to the age your child will complete college (20 or 25 years). Beyond that, if you are a joint homeowner, both parties should have a policy to cover the outstanding debt liability. It covers you so that you are not leaving a financial burden to the survivor where they can ultimately lose the house. The reason I stated joint ownership is because if you are single and you suffer an untimely death, your beneficiary can sell the house and walk away with the difference. You've heard the statement, buy term insurance and invest the difference. Well the reality is that very few individuals invest the difference so you miss the opportunity to purchase insurance when it's the least expensive—while you are young.

So as we were discussing, the mother with three children and a tight budget, term insurance can protect her three children should anything ever happen to mom.

Now is a perfect opportunity to discuss whether to

leave insurance proceeds to minor children. If you are purchasing insurance to replace the potential loss of income to the household, then the answer would be no. If your children are left as the beneficiaries, the money will be held until your children become of age. So, how will this benefit the children when they can't even get to the money? That is an error we often make.

As a professional, when I help a client determine what insurance needs exist, they often determine their desire to obtain enough to replace the current income they are contributing to the household. They also desire to make sure college obligations are met, and possibly pay off the mortgage of the home. However, when leaving money to minors, keep in mind that they will not have access to the money until they turn eighteen, in some cases twenty-one, based on the state the children reside in. Therefore, the money cannot replace what you once provided for them.

For this reason should death occur, the person responsible for the children should be considered to have control of these funds as a need arises. In some cases people can be hesitant about leaving money to guardians and other family members. But what if the parties now responsible for your children were less financially secure than you? What type of environment will your children grow up in? Furthermore, you cannot control your child's life from the grave. We'd like to think our children are all college bound and willing to do anything mommy and daddy might want them to do. Throughout the years in the business, however, I have seen many children turn eighteen, liquidate the assets that their parents earmarked for college, and travel the world in a brand new car. So, let's think about this for a moment. If you were eighteen years old and someone told you there was $250,000 waiting for you, what would be the first thing you would do? Do you want to give your children that option? The decision of who should receive the insurance proceeds is a personal one, but when dealing with minor children, my advice is, if someone is good enough to raise your children they should be good enough for the money. Besides, they need it to raise your children in a similar lifestyle as you would. After all, that's why you chose the person in the first place …you trusted them.

If cost is not an issue or you are in the beginning stages of investing, I would encourage you to consider permanent insurance. A serious misconception is that insurance is not necessary as one matures in age. I beg to differ. If you are successful in accumulating a substantial net worth, you may be subject to estate tax liability and final income tax liability. Permanent insurance will assist you in passing on an inheritance to the next generation. When utilizing permanent insurance, you can also use it as a retirement supplement. Let me explain. First, whole life policies are the most expensive policies available but you will never worry about not getting paid. If you pay when you are alive, when you die, the insurers will pay. You are paying for the comfort in knowing that your policy will ultimately be redeemed. Does this policy make sense for everyone? It depends your age and how sophisticated you are with investments. With an understanding of the securities industry, a variable universal policy or a universal life policy might make sense. A variable policy allows you to purchase insurance and allocate a portion of your premium into mutual funds allowing the growth of the cash value to increase the death benefit of the policy. This cash value can be borrowed and/or withdrawn tax free and will only reduce the death benefit provided the cash value is properly invested. This can serve to be a valuable retirement supplement or college savings vehicle covering two family needs with one payment. If you are not comfortable with investing in the mutual funds, then you may want to consider universal life insurance. The cash value accumulates over time because a fixed interest rate is allocated according to current interest rates. This reduces the investment risk. One note, investing in the financial market has its risks and an investor must understand the risks before allocating money earmarked for insurance into these vehicles. An additional benefit to permanent insurance is that once the policy is purchased, your health no longer becomes an issue. Provided you honor the terms of the policy, you will always be insured.

Once you determine what insurance works best for you, the process does not stop there. Well, what do I mean? Sometimes we think once we have the insurance, we are done. We might get the insurance through our job or take the initiative to get it on our own. We think long and hard about the people we want to have the money should something happen to us. That might be our spouse, our parents, or our children. What we don't consider, is if our circumstances have changed. Divorce is both popular and something most people choose not to discuss with other people. It makes the individual feel like a failure. But by not communicating about divorce, key financial issues relating to the relationship often are overlooked. I am primarily speaking of changing the name of the beneficiary on a policy or a retirement account. Very often I have clients who are on their second marriage. They come to see me with the new spouse to complete a financial plan. As I begin to review the insurance policies, I find that the ex-spouse stands to benefit financially if the client were to die. When the divorce took place, the client never bothered to change the beneficiary on their life insurance policies, especially the policies on the job.

Fortunately I have the capability to change my client's situations, but how many people perish without having that opportunity? Bigger than that, what if you were the surviving spouse? You know your mate has a policy on the job so you go to collect from the employer. But wait, they tell you, "Sorry, you're not the beneficiary and I am not at liberty to disclose the information to you." Now the ex-spouse, who you can't stand, is driving around in a brand new car, wearing a new wardrobe, thinking "I knew he/she still loved me." If your mate wasn't dead, at that precise moment, you could kill them yourself. The sad thing is that this occurs more often than not. How can it be prevented? If you take the time to develop a plan, you must periodically update the plan. This is particularly important when experiencing a life-changing event such as marriage, divorce, death or the birth of a child.

Finally, I implore you to consider the ones you love when making decisions about what insurance would make the most sense for your family. While I cannot answer all of the questions regarding your personal life insurance needs, I anticipate this gives you direction and information that will assist you in protecting your family. After all, we protect everything else in our life—our house and our cars—why not protect your family as well. I know that while I'm alive, I will do whatever I can to provide a wonderful life for my children. If the Lord chooses to take me home while they are still my financial responsibility, I still want to provide them with the best opportunities to succeed in life. Don't you?

A simple blueprint to assess insurance needs is as follows:

Take the age of your youngest child and determine when they will graduate from high school. Multiply that number of years by 80% of your current income. Add the outstanding mortgage liability. If you want to provide for the college needs of your children, determine which college you want to pay for. Add that number into the mix. Use that as a guide of how much life insurance you need.

Measuring Posts

How much life insurance do you have on your job?

How many children do you have?
How old are the children?

What is your annual contribution to the household?

Do you have an outstanding mortgage?

HOW TO GIVE
YOURSELF A BREAK
FROM TAXES

I want to take this time out to say thank you. Thank you to all of the people fortunate enough to make it into middle class America. Thank you to all of the single people with no dependents. The economy is managed off the sweat of your labor. Your tax liability is so great and you can't even take advantage of the tax incentives set aside for you because you don't know what they are. I believe Uncle Sam is entitled to his share of money, but not a penny more. And if you don't know what tax incentives work to your advantage, or you're not astute enough to seek the expertise of a Certified Public Accountant, then I appreciate your willingness to contribute your hard earned dollars to support the land of opportunity. But just for the record, the wealthy do not pay significant taxes compared to their income. Whenever tax laws change, the wealthy hire experts to figure out the loopholes that will allow them to keep the money they make. Quick lesson, it's not what you earn, it's what you keep.

I know a single woman who works everyday, making over $100,000 annually and has no dependents. She does not own a home. She does not have a business. She doesn't have a portfolio or any emergency cash. She doesn't have any habits either: no drugs or alcoholic tendencies and she doesn't gamble. Where is her money going? For one, she is in an extremely high income tax bracket so Uncle Sam takes a significant portion of her earnings between federal and state taxes. Social Security is entitled to its share of her money leaving her with less money to work with. Do you know what she shared with me the first time I talked finances with her? She just started saving in her 401K plan five years prior to our meeting although she had been on her job for almost twenty years. She just thought she couldn't afford a house and she never knew what the maximum allowable contribution was for her retirement plan.

People get to a point in their careers where financially one must evaluate the greatest way to reduce the tax liability. When speaking with this young lady, I stressed to her that if she began to save for retirement alone, the money she set aside through her 401k could serve as a current year tax deduction as well. This was something she desperately needed. A house, or a baby, or all three options were great opportunities to reduce or save on taxes.

So how can you take advantage of tax breaks? Putting money aside for retirement is one good way to start. Even if you make $30,000, if you decided to save three percent of your money for retirement, two things will happen.

First of all, you will save $900 each year. That money will be deducted from your salary earned. So instead of paying taxes on $30,000, your tax liability will be measured by $29,100. This is not taking into consideration any other tax breaks and/ or deductions you may be entitled to. Saving that amount is like taking money out of your left hand and saving it into the right.

Second, you've just started accumulating assets, specifically for retirement. You are now a saver. I'm told the most difficult task in financial planning is starting. So consider this move a major step a person could make toward planning.

I can even think of another incentive. Most people in Corporate America believe they are underpaid. Do you feel that way? Well, many retirement plans in Corporate America promote savings with dollar for dollar or fifty cents per dollar contributing matching incentives. So if you save that same $900 a year, your company will match you by contributing an additional $900 under the dollar for dollar match plan. It's like free money. Now, you have saved $1800 in one year. You've also reduced your tax liability and that sounds like a win-win situation to me!

Let's talk about houses for a moment. A house generally is the most expensive investment minorities tend to make. It's something everyone is entitled to at some point, simply from a comfort level perspective. However is it necessarily an asset? Let's define assets to make that determination. An asset is something that has value. When you purchase a home, usually the amount you owe can be more than what the house is worth when you consider the interest you must pay on the loan. This is even if you purchase the house at a discount, or with equity built in. Therefore, based on the definition, the house is a liability. It very rarely becomes an asset to you. Only when the value of the house is more than the amount you owe on the house including interest does that perspective change.

So what is the benefit of owning a home? When you purchase a house, you receive a mortgage payment. That payment consists of principal and interest. In the very beginning, the interest payments are the majority of your payments. The interest you pay represents a tax deduction for most homeowners. Therefore, if someone is looking for a substantial tax deduction, they may look to purchase a home. However, the miscalculation comes in when people begin to sell their house to buy a bigger house as their salary increases. This is not necessarily the smartest thing to do. I suggest you contact your Certified Public Accountant for advice. I do believe in home ownership. Some things are far more precious than money. The sense of ownership and the emotional component of having a place of your own override financial literacy. I believe it should.

Rich people seem to enjoy the best of both worlds. How is it rich people don't pay taxes or they minimize their tax liability? First of all, many financially successful people are entrepreneurs who have established genuine companies. This is a perfect opportunity to evaluate your gifts and talents. Could a skill you have be turned into a business? Why? Corporate tax liability is dramatically different from personal tax liability. It is less expensive than our highest individual marginal tax bracket. Secondly, within a corporation, expenses are deducted before taxes are paid to the government. Therefore, if you were to have a corporation, it could be possible that the car you need to travel to meetings could be classified as an expense. The dinner tab you picked up when entertaining a client, the computer you purchased to keep your financial affairs in order, supplies you bought to maintain your office. All of these things may serve as justifiable expenses to conduct a business. Your CPA would make that determination based on the type of business you have.

This is a great opportunity to discuss why reduction of your tax liability is necessary. It is an area that you can control. An area that you have no choice is money that is earmarked for OASDI. We are more familiar with the term social security. What is OASDI? It stands for Old Age Survivors and Disability Insurance. It is the official name for the program that gives money raised from payroll tax deductions to retired and disabled citizens. FICA-Federal Insurance Contributions Act is what allows the social security payroll deduction to be collected. It is broken up accordingly; 6.2% represents FICA and 1.45% represents the Medicare tax for a total of 7.65%. This is your contribution. Your employer must match you 7.65% for a total contribution between both parties of 15.3%. And if you are self employed, you are responsible for the latter. One final note, as of 2006, you are only responsible for FICA up to $94,200 of your earnings base. You stop paying once you hit that threshold but there is no limit for the Medicare portion (1.45%).

I know we constantly hear about social security reform and it will not be around much beyond the baby boomer generation, but you still have an obligation to pay. As you can see, the government doesn't give you a choice. The money is withdrawn before you even see your paycheck.

So if you really wanted to minimize your taxes and maximize on your ability to save, take a look at what some financially successful people are doing. I can almost guarantee you they aren't paying a lot of taxes. Once again it isn't what you earn; rather it's what you keep. We, too, should look to keep our money working for us.

Measuring Posts

Get an accountant and stop doing your own taxes. They know more than you do. You are paying them to know all of the tax laws. They change the laws too often for us to keep up.

Check with your employer to see how much money they are contributing to your retirement savings and begin saving at least that.

Identify your gifts and skills. Determine if they could be developed into a business.

SAVE A PENNY TODAY

People always wonder why I do not talk about investments, especially at my seminars. Personally, I've always wanted to separate myself from the belief that a financial advisor is basically a salesperson. Financial advisors have historically been compared to salespeople with a negative emphasis on the description. That is because we work off commission and our advice, as an industry, is subject to what's best for the client. Therefore, many planners will sell clients products they may not need—of course they can *justify* the sale but it doesn't always *benefit* the client. I take offense to the classification because I do not operate that way. I don't "sell" people things. My commitment is to understand a client's needs and goals, and then try to find products that will help them achieve those goals financially. I will refuse a sale if I don't think it benefits a client.

I take great pride in showing people the value of creating their own personal plan of action for their lives. I am an advisor, a true planner. Sometimes, I have people come into my office with the desire to purchase stock and the last thing they need is 100 shares of Cisco or 50 shares of Microsoft. They don't even need to systematically save $100 a month purchasing a quality blue chip mutual fund. Why not? There isn't any money saved anywhere at all. They are one paycheck away from eviction and if something serious were to happen, the first place they would come for money\ would be their investment account. That is a serious problem. When an individual must liquidate a portfolio unexpectedly, they leave themselves vulnerable to possible loss of principal.

My first question to a potential new client is, "If you lost your job tomorrow, do you have three to six months of emergency cash set aside?" The majority of the time, the answer is no. I then ask, "Are you consistently saving any money?" Again, the answer is usually no. I ask, "Are you at least participating in your retirement plan on your job? Do you have life insurance? Health insurance? Do you own your own home?" Before determining if a client can invest, these are just a few questions that need to be addressed.

Until a plan is devised to address those issues, buying stock is not an option. I never object when a client who has not yet begun to accumulate wealth wants to invest. I simply devise a plan that will take care of both their short term needs and their long term desires.

I don't want any of my clients to need money and be subject to market risk and potential loss should an emergency arise. The loss of money in the stock market affects people emotionally and often cripples their behavior when they should be saving. This is why it is very important to understand the basic fundamentals of the stock market overall. No one ever said the market only goes up. Clients must understand that a financial advisor cannot guarantee results nor can they guarantee a client absolutely cannot lose money.

However, giving your investments an opportunity to grow with time can benefit you financially over the long term. As a matter of fact, the stock market historically has been one of the greatest investments available. But you have a responsibility to ensure that you are properly invested, that you understand the risk, and that you have the time. You must be in the position to allow the money to fluctuate with market conditions and not rely upon the investments when you have emergencies.

The key is time!

There is major value in saving and investing at an early age. However, understand there is also a difference between the two. The first step would be to set up a savings plan. When setting up the plan, you are making the decision to set aside money systematically. Within the savings plan, the chance to invest in stocks, bonds, and mutual funds will arise and can be used as a tool to utilize.

There are short term and long term investments. When saving to accumulate the necessary resources for the short term, you are looking at vehicles like cash and cash equivalents such as money market funds or CD's. Short-term investments usually can be liquidated into cash within a year without the possibility of loss to the principal amount.

Because we don't fully understand short-term investments, we tend to think a long term investment is one to two years, if that long. However, when you're seriously putting money away, a long-term investment should be money set aside for an extended period of time giving it an opportunity to grow. The chance to invest in stocks, bonds, mutual funds and other investments increases your ability to be financially free. The decision of what makes sense for an individual to invest in is based on that person's risk tolerance. But then again, that is why a relationship with investment consultants is necessary.

The benefit of starting early, of course, is your money has a longer time to grow. Time adds the greatest value to your investments. You can put aside $100 monthly in a blue chip mutual fund earning 10% interest from the age of 21 until the age of 30. If on your 30th birthday you did not add another dollar, you would have accumulated $17,789.11. By the age of sixty, that money would have accumulated to $310,409.34. For someone who began to save at the age of 30, even if they saved $100 per month earning 10% interest in that same blue chip mutual fund until the age of 45 they would have accumulated $41,21.95 on their 45th birthday. By the age of sixty they would ultimately have $173,865.21. Can you see the value in starting early?

Some of us are somewhat knowledgeable about invest-ments. Therefore, you set up a savings plan and became committed to putting your money in the stock market. Yet you don't open your statements when they come in the mail. This is your responsibility, but it is a major problem in our community. In addition, the investment selection that you make at the age of 25 may be different at the age of 45. When was the last time you evaluated your risk tolerance. Think about it for a moment, when you are young and impetuous, your willingness to take risk is higher—drinking, gambling, partying all night, etc. But ten years later with a different set of circumstances called wife, husband, children, mortgage, you may not be inclined to take unnecessary risks. You have to stay connected.

Let me share with you how I determine who I will work with. When I have an initial consultation, I request statements from the potential clients. I'm generally looking for retirement assets, 401k plans, bank statements, and brokerage accounts. I'll review insurance policies and wills to ensure they are current and consistent with the client's desires. I often find that many people made choices in their retirement plans when they first started the job. After being on the job four or five years, they haven't thought to evaluate their portfolio. They don't take the time to review their statements but they are consistently contributing to the investments. People should use the quarterly statements sent to them by their employers as an opportunity to evaluate their financial status. How do you know if your portfolio needs adjustments if you don't even open the envelope? I look at how connected individuals are with their money, how aware are they of their assets, and if they have a history of being financially reckless. I'm not looking for the perfect client. I'm looking for individuals who want their financial future to be different. Even if you made irrational decisions in the past, your willingness to work with a professional works to your advantage. I request clients prove they are committed. It is not a test, but a necessity. If I give the person a job to do with a time commitment, they show their seriousness by completing the task. Generally I need this foundation to build the plan.

And from the moment we begin to work together, they must open their statements.

Furthermore, how can you get upset with an advisor when you're not even watching your own assets? I can't begin to tell you how many portfolio evaluations I've completed and had to call the new client and say, "I'm sorry, this stock is worthless." Although it took some time for the average stocks to devalue, the client chose to ignore their money despite news heard on TV and the radio that the economy was vulnerable and stocks were not performing well. The people were hoping things would change or go away. Something did go away, their assets.

Recently I contacted a client to discuss her portfolio with her. She was well diversified but her portfolio was suffering along with the rest of the market. After the market began to improve slightly, I wanted to reiterate that her portfolio suited her risk tolerance and there was no need to make adjustments at the time. While speaking with her, she indicated that she hadn't looked at her statements during the past several months. I realized that she represented many clients out in society today. I speak to the individual at least once a month. She is always fully aware of where she stands financially, yet she still did not open her statements.

People sometimes misunderstand their relationship with an advisor. I don't know too many advisors who say they will watch your portfolio and you don't have any responsibility. It is a relationship. You must be committed as well. If your advisor doesn't call you, contact him/her. Don't just allow your money to go down the drain and then blame the advisor saying they didn't advise you.

I know of cases where advisors will contact their clients and the clients will not return the call because they believe the advisor is looking to make a trade. First of all, how would you know if you don't return the phone call? Secondly, if you believe the only time you hear from your investment professional is when they are attempting to sell you something, you need to find someone more suitable to your needs. Find someone who is an advocate for your financial future. But do something …take action.

The best way to handle this is to first be aware of what's going on with your money and your own habits. This allows you to be honest about what changes might need to be made. For example, when you are in a relationship do you share with your mate if you are a saver or a spender? What about your mate? Did you ask? When do you believe is the appropriate time to find out? I don't know if I want to learn about my spouse's spending habits once I'm married with children.

People often ask me how they should approach a conversation with a significant other about money. It is such a sensitive subject. While I agree one should tread lightly, understand this …if you're building a life with someone, you need to know what you are getting into. The last thing you want is someone who is unequally yoked with financial objectives varying so dramatically. You will be in for a ride—and not a ride of choice. But understand this, even if someone has not been successful saving in the past, if they are interested in being progressive and financially free, you can consider moving forward. Once you've determine your spending habits together, you can create a plan of action that suits both of your personalities.

For example, if Michelle knows that her mate Derrick tends to overspend when cash is available, Michelle can avoid financial distress by reducing his available spending cash. Let's say Derrick pays all of his mandatory monthly bills but doesn't save a penny. Michelle can mask Derrick's savings by creating a savings plan and identify it as an expense. Now Derrick is accumulating assets. But here's another scenario. Michelle is one with a passion for the shoe store. She is at the point that she is hiding the bags from Derrick. What can Derrick do to support Michelle's quench for shoes without compromising their joint commitment to save and invest? Together they can make shoe shopping an event with limits. Perhaps a spree four times a year with a limit of the purchase of five pairs of shoes will satisfy Michelle's passion. Not only can she save money, but she doesn't have to give up what she loves to do.

There are even more inspiring reasons people should begin saving. Are you committed to tithing in your local congregation? Tithing is giving 10% of everything you generate back to God. Imagine how rapidly you will accumulate assets if you saved 10% of your income for yourself in addition to what you give back to the Lord. Very often I use that as a blueprint when I speak to different organizations. The Scripture states that if you bring your tithes and offerings to the storehouse, God will pour you out a blessing you will not have room enough to receive (Malachi 3:11). The vehicle you choose to use to save can be blessed. Not all churchgoers subscribe to this ideology. So while you're angry, let me add that miraculous debt cancellation is contrary to the Word of God. Paul interpreted borrowing by indicating that we should owe

THE ULTIMATE PLAN

no man but love. But the broader understanding deals with honoring the taxes imposed by our government, obligations you enter into, and the commitments you make. Let's evaluate this practically. You borrow money for something you desire to have—a house, a car, jewelry. You've enjoyed the benefits but now you don't want to pay. Where is God in that? That type of behavior is a sign of wickedness and it clearly doesn't reflect the character of Christ.

Okay. So let me back up my explanation about Christians not supporting God blessing your savings. Once I gave a seminar to a local Parent Teacher Organization meeting in New Jersey. I stated that if you can tithe, you can save 10% for yourself as well. Now I have always believed in the principle of tithing. I trust God and the Bible in its totality. Speak to any of my pastors since I was a little girl and they can attest to the fact that I've always paid tithes. Now having said that, I shared how God has blessed me in my investments because I was a sound financial steward. I indicated that investments can serve as an area that the Lord proves how mighty He really is. After the seminar was over, a woman approached me because she was distressed that I stated we are responsible for saving for our future. She said I didn't have faith God would bless my tithes and my commitment to saving indicated I felt the need to supply my own needs.

I realize people actually feel that way but would God have us to be ignorant or unprepared? I firmly believe He will not bless you if you're not capable of handling the blessings. He will give you everything you need, including the proper management skills to maintain and

91

appreciate the blessings. He will even give you a plan and people to help you along the way. Even people like me. The seed of information you need to save is all here but God is not going to allow money to fall out of the sky into your living room. He is capable, but I doubt that will happen.

While giving another seminar at a women's ministry retreat, a young lady stated she was taught to save using a 10–10–80 agenda. Pay 10% tithes to God first. Secondly, pay yourself 10%. Finally, the remaining 80% is designated for your expenses. If 80% cannot cover your expenses, you are living beyond your means. Don't worry if you cannot apply that to your life today. Plant the seed, save a dollar today!

MEASURING POSTS

Pay your tithes.

Educate yourself.

Start investing in your retirement first.

Begin early.

SO YOU WANT
TO RETIRE?

One potential client approached me who had been working in corporate America well over thirty years. The individual was concerned about the ability to retire comfortably now that the time was quickly approaching. Because of the state of the economy, many major corporations had been offering long term employees early retirement incentives. One reason for the trend is because if an individual has worked for a company for at least thirty years, the expense of their salary and benefits is comparable to two recent graduates at any average college. Even if the company retired their long term employees, they could reduce the expenses and still maintain quality service. At any rate, this person's employer offered a generous severance package and a pension. The client was fifty years old and walked away with a pension worth approximately $300,000. The client wanted to know if I could help because it was their desire not to work any longer. However she was accustomed to a lifestyle equivalent to $50,000 earning per year. The $300,000 was all she had. She did not take advantage of the 401k available until approximately five years before her retirement. And she had an outstanding loan against the monies that were accumulated. I was very disheartened when the client began to realize that her co-workers were accepting the deal and walking away with a significant pension payout along with an average of $900,000 that had accumulated over the time of their employment through systematic 401k contributions. The client began to understand the missed opportunity. Sadly, I showed several possibilities but the client realized that eventually she would be forced back into the work force. However, we were able to compromise by creating a plan that would allow her several years rest before re-emerging into the workplace.

We often don't think about retirement until it's too late. But a quick note to the entrepreneurs specifically, it is even more essential for you to make sure proper plans are in place. With a major corporation, you may be entitled to some savings. If you step out on faith and establish your own business, you will be faced with responsibilities that employees of a major corporation do not face. As a self-employed person, you must establish your own retirement plan.

People however tend to concentrate so much on the particular business, issues like life or health insurance and retirement planning often go unaddressed. It's easy to allow that to slip through the cracks as your major focus is on running the business. It all seems like so much work. How does one even get started? How do you determine which retirement plan best suits your needs? All of that must be determined based on the financial state of your business, the stability of your income, how many employees you have, and how much you are willing to contribute on the behalf of those employees. The availability of retirement plans are many but those questions will identify what plan you should begin to look at.

For example, if you are a sole practitioner without any employees, you might consider a Simplified Employee Pension or Sep IRA. A Sep IRA is an employer retirement plan that uses IRA's as a funding vehicle. You have the option of putting away more money than allowed in a standard IRA. If you have employees, and they are willing to contribute, yet your company is still very small, you may look at a Simple IRA or a profit sharing plan with a 401k provision. As the employer, you can commit to contributions based on the success of your company in a given year. In addition, with that type of plan, your employees have the option of saving independently. If your business expenses are stable and you want to maximize your contributions, you may consider a money purchase plan. As you can see, because of the various options available, you should consult with your certified public accountant and/or your financial consultant. They would be the best people to better explain the different plans and assist you in determining which plan is for you.

How important and immediate a need is it to save for your retirement? Have you seen a bitter old man working at Target or Wal-mart grumbling to himself about the mess other people left for him to clean up? He's following people everywhere they go complaining about the mess they are making. He realizes that he will be the one responsible for cleaning it up. Now he is not working at a store because it is his desire. This is a clear example of an individual that did not take advantage of saving in small increments when given the opportunity. Despite the thirty years of his life he gave to Corporate America, he did not properly plan for his retirement. Perhaps, he did not take advantage of saving in small increments when given the opportunity. Perhaps he did not protect his assets by diversifying properly or maybe he spent money lavishly without thought for tomorrow, thinking tomorrow will never come. So he now has to continue working at a new company to make ends meet. So he murmurs and complains because he is upset that he has to be there. He does not have a choice.

In that very same store is a beautiful, grandmotherly figure looking fabulous. She is working at the cash register or stationed at the customer service line. She always has a smile on her face and she looks for opportunities to encourage the young teenagers working by her side. You will probably find her advising the girls to stay away from the boys who are inclined to be trouble. She shares wisdom and teaches them how to dress appropriately and encourages them to stay in school. She reflects an individual who *chooses* to work later on in life. When she is prepared to visit her grandchildren for a month, she can just pick up and go. The woman is working simply because she is looking for something to do. Her current employment does not define her financial status. Getting out the house and around others helps her stay young at heart and productive. The salary at this stage in her life does not define her lifestyle. What position do you want to be in? Do you want to be the bitter old man or the nice little grandmotherly figure?

Do you know when you want to retire? What does retirement mean to you?

I began thinking about those questions after turning 30. I truly believe once people hit the "Big 3–0" they begin to concentrate on their accomplishments. Ask yourself, what have I done with my life? Am I happy with where I am today? People begin to evaluate their lives and judge whether they have any measure of success. Are they happy with their careers? Are they financially secure?

At the age of thirty, so many major life decisions are made. People change careers, settle down, start families, get insurance, begin saving and investing. But they should also begin to think about retirement. When I hit thirty, I decided I wanted to be capable of retiring by the age of forty five.

Therefore I had to make commitments toward the things I need to do in order to accomplish that goal. The first thing I evaluated was the type of lifestyle I wanted to live during retirement. Once that was identified, I could put a dollar amount to the desire and make the goal measurable. I now have something to work toward. It is never too late or too early to decide how you want to spend your retirement years. Whatever you decide is totally up to you.

However, I encourage you to think about it now, whether you are twenty-five or fifty-five. What type of lifestyle do you want to maintain and how soon? People are living a lot longer these days. So you must understand it is to your advantage to begin saving today to plan for tomorrow. If you really want to retire financially secure, the best way to achieve that goal is to save a little money each paycheck. The consistent contributions over an extended period of time work in your favor. Also, remember this. If you are accustomed to surviving off of $50,000 annually, you want to save enough money during your working years to support the lifestyle you've developed for yourself. Don't forget that the cost of living will increase as the years pass you by. What will $50,000 today represent twenty years from now?

I need to add one additional thought when considering retirement. People are living much longer in retirement but are not necessarily the healthiest people around. One way to virtually guarantee a life of poverty in retirement is to not address the need for long term care. One illness can significantly diminish whatever savings you have accumulated without proper planning. We will address long term care in the next chapter.

MEASURING POST

Begin to think about your expenses in retirement. Will you still have a mortgage? Do you
intend to move? Do you plan to travel?

Contact social security to determine how
much money you can expect each month.

Communicate with your employer to determine what
type of retirement benefits are available to you.

Contact a financial planner. Your retirement
assets are going to have to last for the remain-
der of your life. You must work with a professional who knows more than you.

ESTATE PLANNING

Nobody likes to talk about death. Therefore most people avoid the area of estate planning because they don't want to think about what will happen when, not if, they die. It is a subject that should be approached sensitively, but approached nevertheless. Think for a moment. When you were a senior in high school, was there a death that really shattered your graduating class? Years later, when you turned 25, you began to hear about old classmates that are no longer around. As you continued to mature, the reality of death begins to sink in and become a way of life.

In addition, it seems that every time you turn around, you can see the evidence of our African American baby sisters and brothers dying younger and younger. Look at Aaliyah, Biggie Smalls, Tupac Shakur, Lisa "Left Eye" Lopez, JoJo from around the way—need I go on. The list is growing. Now you're thirty years old and it's no longer accidents and unfortunate incidents killing your colleagues and friends. Natural causes and health-related issues are the culprit. So when is the right time to start planning for what will happen when you make the transition. When do you come to the realization that tomorrow is not guaranteed?

Let me start by sharing a personal story with you. I wasn't always saved, sanctified and running for Jesus 24/7. As a teenager, I was impregnated at the tender age of fifteen years old. Scared and hiding my deep, dark secret, I did not receive the proper care a pregnant woman needs to birth a healthy baby. When I could not hide the secret any longer, I told my mother who immediately recommended I see a doctor for pre-natal care. My first hospital experience was being rushed to the hospital; labor was induced, resulting in an intense fight to save my life. You see, while I was 27 weeks along in the pregnancy the baby was 18 weeks in size. For nine weeks, the stillborn child was poisoning my system. That was my first real encounter with possible death. Since that time, I have experienced near death at least two additional times (9/11 and the car accident six months later). Now during my first scare, I didn't have anything to distribute to others but the other two times I was a wife, a mother, and a woman with assets.

What is estate planning? Estate planning is the process of accumulating and disposing of an estate to maximize the goals of the estate owner. The various goals of estate planning include making sure the greatest amount of the estate passes to the estate owner's intended beneficiaries, often including paying the least amount of taxes. Additional goals generally include providing for and designating guardians for your minor children and/or disabled adult children. It also includes planning for incapacity—something we don't like to talk about—Long Term Care!

Years ago, when my husband and I were planning to go away, we thought about the well being of our children. It was actually the first time we vacationed without them and we were traveling on a plane. Young parents, we didn't have that luxury until our honeymoon years later. We began to think about the possibilities. God forbid something happened to the both of us, who would we trust our most precious commodity with? Now I have three sisters that I grew up with. I am the second oldest with my older sister being two years my senior. I have another sister one year younger and the baby is ten years my junior. Jesse and I made the decision that when my baby sister turned eighteen, we were going to name her as the guardian of our two children. Now you may be wondering why the baby and isn't that an awesome responsibility. We knew that she would have the love and support she needed from the rest of the family. But we based our decision on how our children are treated now. Anytime my son would visit Grandma's house, I could not send him with any homework because it was guaranteed to return incomplete. I think my mother had a rule that homework could not be done at grandma's house during grandma/grandson time. That was the chance she and the boy had to bond, to grow closer. He was there to be spoiled, not disciplined. I learned not to allow him to go if he had a project. Now my older sister lived out of town and away from the rest of the family.

Auntie Sonji, who is closest to me in age, was the person least likely to remain home. As long as she had transportation, when she rolled out, everyone else rolls with her. Don't even think about sending homework. Now she'll make him do it but she wouldn't check it.

Therefore, Jesse knew that if he disappeared for five minutes, Auntie wouldn't question him. Auntie Sonji's position is "You should have done your homework at home. Get it—homework. Work to be done at your house not mine." Now that Sonji is a mother, her position has changed.

Finally, the baby of the family, Auntie Tanya, would allow him to have his fun, but all work must be completed first. As a matter of fact, if Jesse isn't doing well in school, he can't even go to her house. When he did bring homework to her house, she wanted to review the finished product and her standards are similar to ours. In addition, our lifestyles are similar. She, like my children, prefers to be dressed in the latest fashion while still being financially responsible. With her, I know my children's standard of living would not diminish. Furthermore, their college needs would not be an issue and attendance is mandatory, not a choice or an option. This is the one family member capable of handling a financial windfall and would not squander the money.

Consider the people in your family. Everyone has that crazy brother or sister, aunt or uncle. You know, the one you would not leave your children with even for one hour while you're alive. But without a will, you eliminate your choice. The courts will determine appropriate guardians for your family although it may not be your natural selection. Do you want the system to make that decision for you?

It is also critical to review your will—substitute policies such as life insurance plans, retirement plans, 401k plans and annuities at least annually. Situations and circumstances periodically change. People get married, divorced, and your beneficiaries may pass away. You are creating a bigger headache for the survivors if you do not occasionally review your decisions. Your children, in five or perhaps ten years, could become adults during that time span and you can leave the money directly to them.

Completing an estate plan serves another important purpose. The importance does not lie in the amount of money you have accumulated during your lifetime. Knowing this, I called my mother one day to inquire about any specific gifts she desired to leave to a particular daughter. Four girls, she may want earmark a precious heirloom without stirring up controversy or anger among us. At first she joked that she had a metal box full of problems with my name on it. Clearly that may very well define our relationship. Maybe I gave her so many headaches during her lifetime she wanted to reciprocate the favor even in death. But she indicated that she had several life projects she wanted me to finalize should she never complete them herself.

Additionally, she has a bookcase very special to her made by one of her deceased brothers. He made it when she was in the seventh grade and her dad cherished the shelf until he passed away. My mother made it her business to run to granddaddy's house to retrieve the bookcase before it could be permanently damaged. She has enjoyed it for almost forty-five years and counting. Now she wants to pass it down to her first grandchild—my son—because she knows he will take very good care of it. Now to our knowledge, the shelf has little or no monetary value but it is precious and dear to mom. The sentimental value is priceless. The best way to ensure that her first grandchild receives the bookcase at mom's death is for her to include the request in her will. How would anyone know about the special bookcase if we didn't take the time out to ask?

Identifying who you desire to have certain items in a will also eliminates the scavenger hunt that is sure to take place after a funeral. Imagine with me for a moment. Can you recall a family member passing away? The first person to get to the house had their choice of what "goodies" they would take. So many family fallouts follow death. The house was raided by family or something important came up missing. Now my mother has always stated that she never wants to see her daughters fighting amongst each other. Her desire is for us to love each other or at least pretend we do until she is gone. Now, we are all very close but we probably still would fight over certain of my mother's assets. Although my family would not take it personal at the end of the day, families are destroyed with the same circumstances. I'm not saying people will not be disappointed by certain decisions, but at least everyone will know clearly what the deceased wanted others to have.

Finally, we share money with relatives without understanding the consequences to our actions. Well, what do I mean? Recently a client received a lawsuit settlement from an unanticipated death of a family member. The rightful owner of the settlement decided to share the wealth with her children. I explained several options to this client. The first option was that she could give a stated dollar amount without regard for taxes each year. It is classified as an annual exclusion. However, the attorney gave her the option of having the settlement paid to the children directly and she preferred that option. I wanted to be sure she understood the money now belonged to the children. That is what she wanted. Here is where things got sticky. The kids deposited the money back into the mother's account to clear the assets. Unknowingly, they gifted the money to mom which technically gave them no rights to the money. Subsequently, a potential problem existed when they made the decision to put the money back into mom's name. If the deposit was greater than the annual exclusion amount, the gift giver is responsible for informing the government that you made a gift that should be applied to your lifetime credit available to offset gift and estate taxes. The credit allows an average individual to gift in life or death $2,000,000 of their estate without federal estate tax consequences. Therefore, in the example above, if the mother were to give away $200,000 during her lifetime beyond her annual exemptions, she would still have $1,800,000 to give away at death without being subjected to estate tax. The gift excludes the spouse because property transferred to a spouse during life or death generally passes free of gift and estate tax—if they are a citizen of the United States. Different rules apply for non-citizens. Now the mother may have a responsibility to report the gift to her children so she would need to consult the attorney to determine her next course of action. This would eliminate any future potential discrepancies and avoid any complications with the continual transferring of assets.

How does this relate to estate planning? When a person is deceased, a final tax return must be filed. If you accumulate substantial assets and you don't take advantage of proper estate planning tools, you could pay taxes in excess of 45% even in your death. Therefore, a great portion of the money you accumulated during your lifetime can be paid to Uncle Sam, not your beneficiaries, without proper planning. Insurance proceeds are included when determining your individual net worth. So if you accumulated $700,000 in investments and personal property, $500,000 in insurance policies, and a house valued at $500,000 by the age of 65, when you ultimately pass away years later, your estate could be well over $2,000,000 creating a potential problem. If that mom were to die while the money of one of her children was still in her account and her will left her estate to all of her children equally, the one child would be out of luck.

Now don't be hasty in trying to preserve your assets without thinking. I know many people who are not married, get a windfall of money, and deposit the assets into a joint account. This account might be with a significant other, a parent, or a child. However, that other party has just been gifted half of the windfall.

Another hasty decision occurs when parents add their children onto their accounts. Usually they will go to a local bank and establish a joint account with the daughter or son who lives the closest. The reason behind the decision is so that someone can have access to money should the parent become ill or unable to handle the financial affairs from day to day. Here is the problem with that. Let's say you have three children James, Sandra, and Michael. Sandra helps you with everything. She takes you to the store, does your banking, and takes you to the doctor, whatever you need. You want to make life easier for her so you give her access to all of your accounts. You made the decision out of convenience but it was your intention to distribute your estate equally when the time came. One problem, you already gave the money to Sandra. The moment you added your daughter's name, she become the rightful owner of the money with the ability to withdraw out of the account anytime. There is nothing that James and Michael can do. In addition, Sandra is still entitled to her fair share of the estate outside of what she received as a result of being a joint owner with rights of survivorship.

Let me take this time to address additional benefits to comprehensive estate planning. It doesn't just include a will. One should also complete a health care proxy and a power of attorney. The health care proxy clearly outlines what type of medical treatment you desire should you become incapable of making that decision yourself. You have the ability, while you are of sound mind, to outline the type of care you deem appropriate for you. It also takes the pressure off of your loved ones to make difficult choices about the level of care you would desire. Equally as important is the power of attorney. This is also the direction an individual should take when they have multiple children that they want to equally distribute their assets to. A power of attorney is a written instrument which authorizes one person to act as another's agent or attorney. The power of attorney may be for a definite, specific act, or it may be general in nature. The terms of the written power of attorney may specify when it will expire. If not, the power of attorney usually expires when the person granting it dies. Remember the mom with the three children James, Sandra, and Michael? The mom can give Sandra power of attorney granting Sandra the ability to act on her behalf while still preserving her intention of equal distribution of her estate amongst her children.

Please allow me to go back to a need for a health care proxy. When identifying specifically the level of care you desire, this is a perfect opportunity to address long term care needs. A person, as they grow older, may not be as capable of maneuvering as effectively as when they were in their thirty's, forty's and fifty's. Long term care represents medical, social and personal care services, such as nursing home care, home and community based care, hospice care, or respite care, required over a long period of time by a person with a chronic illness or disability. If you do not address these needs during the implementation of an estate plan, you may not have an estate to distribute. Why? Because the rising costs of long term care needs over time can diminish any modest estate. This is an area in which you must familiarize yourself with your particular state law and what provisions are available to you based on your net worth. But I will give you a word of caution. Creating a long term plan that includes giving your money away to make yourself eligible for Medicaid is not a sound strategy. The tax laws are constantly changing. Because of the rising costs, your best option is to evaluate your net worth at the time of retirement, if you haven't considered Long Term Care insurance beforehand.

I want to address one more example of a hasty decision people tend to make. It is when you put money in your children's name. You may set up a custodial account classified as a Uniform Gift To Minors Act or a Uniform Transfer To Minors Act. Once money is put into a child's name, you have no personal right to the money. Any monies taken out of the account before the age of majority, 18 or 21, depending on which state you reside in, should be used for the benefit of the child. In more detail, the account is designed to allow a relatively simple method of making gifts to minors of certain property (securities, cash, life insurance, and annuities, to name a few) without court supervision. The account is set up with an adult acting as a custodian for the minor. The adult is given broad investment powers under the "prudent person" standard. The custodian has the ability to spend property on the behalf of the minor without a court order.

People argue with me about this point all of the time. They say, "The bank is allowing me to take the money out." That is not the purpose of the account. Finally, all of the money must be given to the child outright by the age of majority.

As an individual developing an estate plan, you have the opportunity to designate things that are important to you to the people you really want to have them. You can and should make those decisions while alive, healthy and in your right frame of mind. Additionally, you want to be well informed of all decisions you make and the potential problems that could arise as a result. Otherwise, start turning over in your grave, calamity is about to fall. If you fail to plan, you will plan to fail.

Measuring Posts

Do you have a will, a power of attorney, and a health care proxy?

What lifestyle would you like your family to maintain should you die prematurely?

What plans do you have in place should you suffer a long term illness?

Who do you trust to raise your children?

REVELATION

Early one Saturday morning when I began to read pages of the book originally written when I turned 30, I wasn't sure what God was trying to show me. But on that day, I discovered *the* assignment or mission God had for my life. I thought it was my purpose, but five years later, I recognize that it is a piece of what I do and not completely who I am. I promise to elaborate on that revelation later. It was mind blowing what poured out of my spirit once I started typing. Understand how powerful it is to write the vision and make it plain. I knew I was being called to empower and educate my community about financial planning. Our issue in this area was great. I knew by the end of that year, I would have to make dramatic changes in my life. I had always known that I was going to make a profound impact in my community, but I wasted precious time walking into my destiny. My first step would be to terminate my relationship in the partnership that I had been in for over eight years. I was restless but it was through my writing that I was able to identify where to start.

Focusing on three potentially vulnerable areas within

the African American community became my concentration. The youth, the entertainment industry, and our churches was my original focal point. It became clear to me that if those areas were adequately impacted, a significant change could take place socially in the mindset of our culture. Now that was *my* original thought. I learned through trial and error, and based on my success and/or failure, God's focus was the youth, our churches, and the penal system.

To begin with the youth, I had to get close to them first. I knew I needed to present my proposal to the Board of Education to even be considered. This is normally not an easy task. The public school system is often difficult to penetrate. Sometimes even the best programs are rejected for any number of reasons. Suburban school districts were already offering their children proper money management information. Why not provide our students in urban district communities with the same opportunity to be financially sophisticated?

For me to do the will of God, especially after sparing my life, I had no choice but to find a way to infiltrate the school system, even if I had to dedicate my time and expertise for free. That's when I met Sergeant DeLacy Davis. He helped me get my foot into the door. So let me give you a little background. I spoke to DeLacy before September 11th and we set a meeting for the last week in September. I invited him out to lunch because he was a community leader and I thought he was someone I needed to know. DeLacy was the first person I spoke with after the tragedy and he was prepared to cancel the meeting because he knew I worked at the Trade Center. I would not even consider it—I was on a mission. By the end of the luncheon meeting, I had a commitment for the first school I would be teaching in. It was not an interest but a firm commitment. Together we submitted a proposal to the Board of Education to teach the students about finances. Not only was it immediately accepted by the board, but his chief also indicated that the financial proposal was the best idea DeLacy offered to the school system. Armed with that confirmation, I had the ammunition I needed to target other urban district schools.

This afforded me the opportunity to go into several schools once a month to teach the basic fundamentals of finances and investments. The response in the first year was so overwhelming that students in different schools approached their principals and teachers. I realized the value in the program when I began to receive phone calls from several parents requesting information about upcoming seminars. Parents were very happy that their children were learning these valuable tools. Very often I would hear, "I wish someone was teaching me this when I was in high school. I definitely would have made different choices in life."

Teaching our children everything they need to know about money is essential if we are going to get ahead. The urban school district curriculum teaches them about stocks, bonds, and mutual funds. I found it equally important to review goal setting and to talk about credit. Not just what credit is, but also the difference between good credit and bad credit. We discuss how the economy affects the stock market, the importance of saving, and men versus women and their relationship with money. We dispelled the myths about the responsibility of a man and a woman in a relationship. Most of the young people appreciate learning why FICA is taking so much money out of their paychecks from the after school job they are fortunate to have. (I personally did not learn about the importance of social security until I was an adult although I began working as a freshman in high school.) The benefits from the pleasure of teaching, the opportunity to watch children finish college, begin working and create businesses is something that I look forward to any day now. Changing the attitudes of our children towards money can only be successful with our commitment to things being different in our community. If we grew up in an environment where mommy pays for the rent every other month, or that the parent lives from paycheck to paycheck, children are inclined to adopt those habits …unless the chain is broken. Just think about it. Where would you be if you learned about the importance of living within your means? What if you learned about saving for retirement even at the age of 22?

Our young adults should realize that even if they save a minimal amount of money for retirement, they are reducing their current tax liability and saving to build a nest egg. Their greatest advantage to being rich is the time they have to accumulate wealth.

Parents too can play an active role in instilling these ideas into their children. Most people get their first job while still living at home. Therefore, a great opportunity to implement a plan of action becomes available at an early age. A young adult can save money before moving out. How? Most parents do not charge their children rent once the kids reach an age of majority and/or graduate college. But in reality, it is virtually impossible to live anywhere rent free. If mom and dad's rent or mortgage averages $1400 monthly, the newly employed, independent graduate can contribute $400 to the household expenses. To live away from home, it would cost an average individual at least $900. To become accustomed to managing expenses, the daughter or son can save the difference. What will this do? This habit will help create a nest egg. If continued for two years, that young adult could accumulate $12,000 in savings, not including the interest. That is enough money to move out. Also, you are now accustomed to paying that said amount out each month. This is a win-win situation. There is a benefit for parents who often sacrifice to provide a better environment for their kids and also prepares the next generation for the future.

One disconcerting thought is that our youth are continually exposed to small business owners that do not live in the community. It is sometimes difficult to see great examples of successful entrepreneurs that we can aspire to be like. Culturally, it often appears that everyone else is making money but Black folks. You have the Chinese store, the Spanish bodega, the Middle Eastern owned gas stations and other businesses in the average urban community that don't reflect the culture. Sure you have beauty salons, day care centers, and barber shops. But is that enough? Mentorship is critical to our youth becoming successful and we need representation in every career.

But for those who do not see themselves walking down the path of becoming an entrepreneur, it is very important that we realize that we are all independent money managers. You are a business. Your business might be that you are a receptionist, a dental assistant, a caterer or a teacher. Even if you are employed in Corporate America, you must sell yourself to your potential employer and negotiate how much your compensation will be. Most people determine if they can accept a job based in specific, personal needs. Would you take a position that pays you minimum wage if your salary is less than the cost of the transportation to the new job? What if your paycheck only covered the cost of child care? Our youth should begin to see that taking a position that does not meet minimal needs is not a sound business decision.

Unfortunately, the youth often gets their perception of money from the entertainment industry. Television is a powerful tool that gives certain people unmerited respect. Several of the artists in the entertainment industry have a hold on the youth simply because kids can turn on the TV and see their favorite entertainer showing off a house or driving a car that simply doesn't belong to them. The myths need to be dispelled.

I thought to get through to the teens I could utilize some of my connections to the entertainment industry. At the time, I was the host of music video show that allowed me access to many of our favorite hip hop and R&B artists. I felt that my relationship with these artists could be used to my advantage. My primary objective was to capture the attention of the youth. It worked. Every time I began a new session, I would first show the class pictures of me along with some of the hottest artists on the streets right now. Then I would begin to talk about the material things the artists talked about and showed on their videos. Once I had their undivided attention, I could expose them to possible ways they can obtain things important to them without having to be a rapper, singer, actor or sports entertainer. But what I realized early on in the process was that I didn't need a gimmick. As adults, we should trust that the younger generation is an intelligent breed. They want to know how they can "make that paper." They desire the "phat" cars and nice "cribs." As a matter of fact, they have more pressure to represent than we ever did. Anyone sharing valuable information to assist them in a viable financial plan will have their undivided attention. They ask questions about financial prosperity I wish we would have asked years ago.

Understanding the influence that stems from the industry, I began to realize how financially ignorant our artists are as well. They too require education. Their spending habits are often reckless and irresponsible with little or no thought for tomorrow. With my entertainment background coupled with my financial expertise, one glaring red flag is what they do with a lump sum of money not truly understanding that may be the only payday for any given project.

Sometimes an advance is received but it's required to honor commitments. Therefore, if an artist received an advancement of $100,000, immediately taxes should be set aside. Why? First and foremost, future payments are often contingent upon the success of the project. If the project doesn't do well, you may not receive another penny. Now the advance that is given is often designated for various expenses. Just to name a few, production of the product, video promotion, management fees, personal expenses, etc. Therefore, if the artist had created a plan when he/she signed a contract, they would have put themselves on a budget.

If these artists were on a plan or budget, they would own their houses, lease, finance or outright purchase their cars directly, find their accountants and attorneys independently, and make different decisions. Being young and ignorant about the ways of the industry makes them vulnerable. They don't realize if the record company leases the car for you, then you don't own the car. If the record company secures the mortgage for you, you don't own the home. If the record company provides the accountant and the attorney, you will pay top dollar for advice and services you probably don't need. Additionally, they may subconsciously keep the interest of the record company on their mind. But if you found your own support team, they will have your best interest at heart.

Most importantly, entertainers must cover the costs for everything. Again, to avoid future problems with the IRS, the first thing that should be taken out of the money is the taxes because you will be liable. This must be done when the resources are available. Uncle Sam generally is not very patient and he wants his money right away. Without setting aside the necessary funds, when tax season approaches, the entertainer is left in a compromising position. Often it's the beginning of the end for many. The decisions made when the first check is received sets the standard for how the artist will react to money. Wise choices will allow him to maintain a comfortable lifestyle. Shopping, spending excessive cash just to floss, and purchasing depreciable assets will assist in one's financial downfall.

Other issues entertainers face are based on the fast life they live. Money comes and money goes. Very often, they spend, spend, spend because the checks keep coming. I know I would get very comfortable making money hands over fists. Entertainers fall into a false sense of security believing they will always be on top making significant dollars. The reality is that an artist is as hot as their last album. There is no guarantee that the new album will generate the same income as any previous projects. Look at Ja Rule, Ashanti, Vanilla Ice, Mc Hammer, Michael Jackson. Entertainers cannot make the decision to begin saving after the next album.

Consequently, fame comes long before the fortune. But knowing this, why portray having the bling bling, the Hummers and the Bentleys with multi-million dollar cribs if you still live in the hood barely making ends meet?

I realized quickly that any attempts to infiltrate the entertainment industry would be met with opposition. One must be prepared to take on media giants who help create images in our community, both positive and negative. You must have more than one voice to begin making a difference. But the experience with entertainers awakened my eyes to another population; the penal system.

Now I know you might be wondering why anyone would spend their time attempting to financially educate incarcerated individuals. Well, at a time when our artists, corporate executives, and actors/actresses are spending time behind bars and coming out with a greater celebrity status before the incarceration period, we need to be mindful they are truly indeed a select few. Begin to imagine how powerful of an impact we can make if we provide inmates with training in a career and/or skill that would allow them to support their family even with a criminal record. If they are employable, they are less inclined to commit additional offenses that can potentially put them back behind bars. I am not whimsical in this thought. I've had the privilege to work with people with a checkered past. And if we told the truth, some of our past actions should have landed us in a jail. But by the grace and mercy of God, we didn't travel down that road. Now job certification isn't the only missing piece of the puzzle. We must, in reality, provide men and women with treatment programs that will address any potential illness and/or diseases they face. I'm talking about substance abuse, anger management issues, and victims of sexual abuse. Going through those experiences without counseling creates low self esteem and lack of self worth. Therefore, reckless behavior tends to follow. If we can provide someone with a second chance, not only will they become productive citizens in society, they will not return back into the penal system, hereby reducing the recidivism rate overall.

Finally, I had a major desire to extend my expertise to the churches. Boy, if I knew then what I know now, I don't think I would have desired that assignment. But nevertheless, I would have moved forward. The church is probably one of the most challenging institutions to infiltrate, even more so than the school system. It is an area where who you know outweighs what you know. I have found that the average church feels as if they don't need empowering. The average church is perfect. So then why are so many church folks "broke"? I believe this is a question that needs answering sooner than later, especially if we look at the state of the churches in the urban community.

Although I am aware that it is an individual's responsibility to handle their affairs financially, there are questions to consider. Should the church have a responsibility to feed the congregation spiritually and support them in their walk with God in practical areas such as physical, mental and financial areas as well? If your pastor promoted economic empowerment from the pulpit supported by scripture, would you listen? Is everyone in the church financially free? Is the church contributing to the community in the same proportion that the community is contributing to the church?

I started analyzing our beliefs and noticed that people identify mostly with the scripture that states if we suffer, we will also reign with God. The truth of the matter is this. The Bible clearly indicates if we fulfill the requirements of God's Word, including obedience, we will be blessed in every aspect of our lives and our children will be blessed and our children's children. It is the promise of our Father. To me, that means we should not remain poor emotionally, spiritually, or financially. I am not passing judgment on the church but certain things must change for churchgoers to become more progressive. Or we will be in the community, but closed off from the needs of the people.

While moderating an episode of the X Factor, a teen talk show in the state of New Jersey, the youth touched on their attitude toward churches. Their frustration lies in the fact that there is a church and a liquor store on virtually every corner in the average community. The challenge is that the liquor stores are open late but the church doors are often shut. They expressed that perhaps with options, their choices *could* be different. They also expressed discontent with not being heard, constantly being talked about but not having a voice to express their side. They feel that negative social issues can be positively addressed through peer mediation and available recreation. If the youth could occupy their time proactively, they would have limited opportunity to get into mischief. I would interpret that as the youth saying if the church doors were opened as long as the liquor stores, maybe, just maybe, they would choose the church. I fondly remember Friday nights at my church growing up. I'm not saying that churches don't provide that recreation, but it's clearly not being advertised where the youth on the street hang.

Similarly, how unfortunate would it be to have a goldmine of an opportunity available to the church that is never revealed? I believe the church has a responsibility to listen to or review a proposal that lines up with Biblical principles to determine if it is beneficial for their particular congregation. I was extremely devastated when I realized that I was commissioned to "do God's will" but no one wanted to even listen to me. Why? Because the church is built on volunteerism, lack to true commitment, and members of the church being considered "outsiders" looking to infiltrate. Great opportunities are often overlooked.

Let me help someone who works in church administration out, if not for the good of the church, then for your own personal maturity in your Christian walk. The average, everyday person looks at church as a business. If I call you, I expect to receive a call back. This is common courtesy. If you volunteered to become the church secretary, that means you are responsible to respond to what you might even consider a silly phone call. Feeling ignored is a primary reason so many individuals are disgruntled with the church. There is a belief that the average church organization is a taker and not really willing to give. I have personally, in the beginning of my career, contacted hundreds of churches who never responded, even five years later. What's worse, one day I unwittingly left my name *Minister* Nicole Simpson and I received a call back the same day. I was happy to receive the response but disheartened that I had become a priority because of my title. I have never been one to flaunt a ministry title and I never clouded my ability as a planner with the call on my life. As a matter of fact, I find it to be a problem that we judge our sisters and brothers from a spiritual perspective when dealing with business. That is not always the best decision. While any approach to "church folks" needs to be spiritually based, it must be balanced with expertise in whatever field of business you are in. Too often, our churches have difficulty identifying expertise. I found members in the congregation enter into a "spiritual" relationship with "a professional" not a business relationship.

This is a true story. When I first decided to enter into the securities industry, because I was rooted and grounded in the church, I incorporated into my business plan that my sisters and brothers in Christ would be the very individuals that I could assist financially. I am not alone in that thought. The initial exposure that African Americans have to financial consultants is often based on a church member being hired for a new position. The new hire then attempts to build a practice starting with people they fellowship with. In order for a trainee to keep their job, they are required to establish a set number of relationships within a stated period of time. The problem is that most rookies don't quite have experience and they generally burn their first group of clients. So if your first clients are church members, then they've had a bad experience because they didn't take the time out to ask about your expertise and you didn't properly take care of your sisters and brothers in Christ. Now, because I never really had deep roots within my church and I didn't have family members with major responsibility in my church, I didn't have that luxury—thank God. I say that because I also didn't have time to educate while attempting to build a business. My initial thought was that I wanted to stay in the business and the church just wasn't working for me as quickly as I needed it to. But I'm one person. When people get burned, especially in church, they blame the entire black race instead of the individual who used them as a training tutorial. So when I came full circle, with a mandate by God, I faced challenges, because I also didn't have the necessary relationships I needed.

So of course there were many days that I wanted to give up on the church because they weren't responding to "my expertise." I had education, spiritual maturity, and most important, an assignment from the Lord. Why couldn't the church see that I was here to help? So I kept trying, kept calling, kept moving forward. And then I woke up. My mandate was to educate the body, not build a business off of the church. We must clearly define what God is saying to us. As a result of my awakening, I decided that educating the church would become a part of my reasonable service. No strings attached; no expectations. There were too many things our people needed to know. I knew the blessings were certainly there but we must acquire the knowledge. The Word says we are destroyed for lack of knowledge (Hosea 4:6).

With this new outlook, suddenly friends in outside communities began to support me once they heard about my call to ministry and my willingness to teach. They would ask their pastor if I could come into the church to give a free seminar addressing the importance of financial planning and investing. While speaking at one particular church, I received revelation that the seminar would be the basis of even this book. In addition, the assistant pastor of that particular church became my client. Three years later, the Lord called him to pastor and he is my pastor today. Now I've been blessed to speak on local, regional and national platforms.

There are requirements and mandates that God places on us that we must honor. We are all responsible as individuals, but as Christians we have a responsibility to each other as well. What can you do to support your sisters and brothers in Christ? How can you assure them that you operate with a standard of excellence in business as well as ministry? When you really think about it, it's the trick of the devil to have you so caught up in your bills. He wants to keep you distracted so you cannot truly dedicate service and time to the Lord. If you can go to church to grow spiritually, you should learn how to mature financially, emotionally, and physically as well. You should learn from others in your surroundings so that you know how to look for a new job, how to cut unnecessary expenses, or when to step out on faith to establish that new business. All these things are connected and so are we, ultimately desiring the same things and moving forward together as a unified body.

MEASURING POSTS

Begin to think about a time in your life when
you realized the path you were traveling would
not lead you to where you were attempting to go in life. How did you respond?

Do you believe in starting over? Moving
forward? Changing direction?

What is the Lord saying to you?

What is your life's purpose?

A REASON, A SEASON, AND A LIFETIME

Events occur in our lives affecting us for a reason, a season, and sometimes a lifetime. Understanding the reason why the events occur, the proper time it takes to accomplish our desires, and the purpose or meaning we attach to our lives can shape who we are as people. My being at the World Trade Center was for a reason. I had to be at Battery Park City on September 11, 2001. I was there to see firsthand that the wealthy had provisions in place for disaster. They didn't wait until they were faced with tragedy to prepare for the unexpected. When calamity arose, they were in a better position to deal with life's obstacles. That experience allowed me to clearly define my responsibility to promote economic empowerment within my community.

As a result of my near death experience, I decided that the way of the Lord was the only way for me. I realize that everything that happens, happens for a reason. People purchase insurance for a reason. Should something happen to them, their family is protected. They also complete a will for a reason. That reason is to properly distribute their assets as they wish. Some people try to identify the reasons why certain people have entered their life. Are they in my life for a reason?

The Lord certainly put people in my life for a reason. I never really thought about my relationships until after the tragedy. There was one man in particular that comes to mind. He was running for Congress and he requested my support. I had never been involved in a political campaign on any level. Shortly after the experience several people approached me interested in running for office. Now that I have experience in politics, it represents another way the Lord can use me. He paved the way for me to gain experience in that position and I was validated. My relationship with incarcerated women was for a reason as well. It helped me to understand how to effectively minister and teach people about finances with the most challenging circumstances.

Evaluate your life. Can you think about things that happened to you that you can't explain? Or people who came into your life at a particular moment? What was your reaction? Did you dismiss them or did you realize everything occurs for a reason? People will often pass through your life to edify it for a moment. Knowing the particular reason sometimes enables us to accomplish the unattainable and get through the unimaginable.

Likewise, identifying the seasons, or periods in life, when we experience change it enables us to determine how to handle unexpected and difficult situations. So many things can happen during a season. People mature, evolve, and grow in character. There could be a period of time in your life that you must put your desires on hold because of responsibilities. Very often people have children and change the directions of where they were trying to go with their careers. They may work at a job to make ends meet instead of pursing a dream. Parents raise their children for a season. We maintain relationships for a season. Most of us don't know when a season is over and it's time to let go.

When I look at measuring points in my life to identify several seasons, the first one that comes to mind is the five years following my experience at the World Trade Center. It is my belief that we will grow as a person during a season. Our behavior will change and greater character can be developed. For me, I learned how to completely rely upon God for my very sustenance. I began to embrace the call on my life and I believe I submitted to the period of testing that was sure to follow any individual willing to let go and let God. During that season, what was expected of me was revealed, people were removed from my life, and miracles occurred. I've had seasons where I was capable of saving so much money. I've had seasons where every investment I made was sound, every material possession I desired was obtained. I've had seasons where I couldn't determine where my next meal was coming from. I experienced seasons where physically I thought I was knocking at death's door and seasons where I wished I was already there. But in the midst of every season, I began to realize that they don't always last and regardless of the season, I was always blessed.

Just as people come into your life for a reason, they

sometimes come only for a season as well. Have you ever had a powerful encounter with someone who you just met but you felt as if you knew them forever? Immediately after September 11th, I tried to ignore the fact that I needed counseling. Eventually I went back to work and decided to focus on my relationship with God believing whatever process of healing I needed would take place through fasting, praying and studying the Word. However, I was in a serious car accident and I totaled my car. Then my favorite aunt passed away, and every dime my family accumulated for years, was gone. At some point, I knew I needed counseling. I went to a regular counselor, group counseling, and a Christian counselor. Nothing worked. Then someone visited my church. Initially, I didn't really get involved with her, but God has a way of orchestrating certain things. I recall telling her not to look at me because I felt she could look right through me. One day I asked my pastor if she could counsel me because I felt that I had major issues I needed to deal with because my overall growth was being hindered. I felt comfortable with her because she didn't know me and her relationship with God appeared strong. My intense relationship and counseling period was for a season. During that time, I became clear about the journey God was taking me on. We remained friends for a spell but I was always clear that our relationship was seasonal.

Finally, to define a lifetime, you have to have a vision. What would you like to accomplish in your lifetime? What type of impact would you like to have on society? Whether your life is about establishing financial security, setting career goals and achieving them, or building a family all of those things require planning. Financially speaking, one must save to maintain an acceptable standard of living for a lifetime. Tell me when you are going to die and I can tell you exactly how much money you need. Since we don't know, we must make infinite provisions. The earlier you begin, the lesser amount you have to contribute annually. The longer you delay, the more out of pocket expenses you have to dedicate to your lifetime provision.

When I think of lifetime, I think of my desire to be with my husband until death. I desire to share experiences with my children for a lifetime. But most importantly, I pray my relationship with God is a lifetime relationship that will continue to grow and blossom as each day goes by. This, along with any other lifetime objectives, cannot happen without planning and commitment to making it work. It can be physical, mental, emotional or spiritual. If we can start by identifying the reason, the season, and the lifetime events in our lives, we can accomplish what we desire.

Measuring Posts

God uses people to impact your life at different intervals. Identify one person who had a profound impact in your life for a reason, a season, and a lifetime. It does not have to be the same person for each experience.

Where do you go from here?

What commitment could you make to other individuals as they attempt to achieve their life purpose?

What do you require from others to achieve your life purpose?

EPILOGUE

When I realized God called me to the ministry, it became evident that everything I had accomplished in the past needed to be placed on the back burner. Everything I thought defined me, identified me, represented me needed to be stripped. Originally I thought that my purpose was being a minister with a financial stewardship assignment. But as the time passed, I realized that ministry was paramount. I have been called to be an Evangelist. The Lord was commanding me to preach and teach the gospel. To whom much is given, much is required they say. I will say this to anyone who believes they have been called. As I meditated on the call, I began to realize that I operated in the office long before I acknowledged the assignment. Before I declared to the Lord, yes, I walked as an evangelist and I worked as an evangelist.

But naturally, my first reaction was "Why me Lord? This is too much!" Working with people to strengthen their financial lives wasn't enough? But then I remembered my declaration: for God I live and for God I would die. I've had too many encounters with death not to realize the hand he had on my life. So I was tested almost immediately. Financial devastation hit my household after eighteen months of minimal production. The family business tanked because I chose not to be the face of the company any longer. And for the first time since my childhood, I felt hopeless and vulnerable, afraid that I would not succeed. However, in the midst of my uncertainty, my family learned firsthand how God will supply your every need.

For a long time, the difference between my needs and wants could not be clearly defined. But every time I felt I was on the wrong path, God showed just a little of Himself to remind me that his hand was on my life every step of the way. Every day, I thought my husband's patience would wear thin because I was not contributing financially to the household as I did previous years. To make matters worse, I was back to working long hours six days a week and I jeopardized Jesse's ability to provide for the family.

But because of the calling and assignment on his life, Jesse carried the family while I was isolated in the wilderness. My prayer is that God will grant him the desires of his heart, transforming the business in ways I could never envisioned. The season of lack helped me to strengthen my relationship with my Father.

I know who I am based on, who God has called for me to be. I am committed to you, my sisters and brothers. Whatever it takes to strengthen our culture, to bring back family values, to assist people in being financially prepared for anything, and most importantly, to win souls for the kingdom. I am available.

I tell you this story for a reason. I traveled a long road

to get to this place. It is my ultimate trust in God that made me change the direction of where I was going. God is telling some of you to step out on faith. That is the key to your financial freedom. I don't know what that means to you, but if you trust in the Lord, He will carry you through. God might be telling you to go back to school, apply for that new job, create a budget, and stop being irresponsible. Whatever he is saying to you, just do it!

Mathematical Calculations

Client invests $100 monthly in a blue chip fund with a rate of return of 10% for 9 years. The client begins to invest at the age 21 with $0.00 dollars invested and ends at the age 30.

$0.00 Present Value
$100.00 Payment Monthly
9 years
10% Interest
$17,789.11 Future Value

Client stops contributing $100 monthly in a blue chip mutual fund and allows the money to grow from the age 30 until the age 60 with a rate of return of 10%.

$17,789.11 Present Value
$0.00 Payment Monthly
30 years
10% Interest
$310,409.34 Future Value

Client invests $100 monthly in a blue chip fund with a rate of return of 10% for 15 years. The client begins to invest at the age of 30 with $0.00 dollars invested and ends at the age 40.

$0.00 Present Value

$100.00 Payment Monthly

15 Years

10% Interest

$41,621.95 Future Value

Client stops contributing $100 monthly in a blue chip mutual fund and allows the money to grow from the age 30 until the age 60 with a rate of return of 10%.

$41,621.95 Present Value

$0.00 Payment Monthly

15 years

10% Interest

$173,865.21 Future Value

The future value was calculated using a HP 12C.

ABOUT THE AUTHOR

Nicole B. Simpson is a Certified Financial Planner® (CFP) and Certified Senior Advisor® (CSA) with almost 16 years of experience in the securities industry. As a financial consultant with an extensive operational background, she specializes in comprehensive financial planning, including portfolio management, retirement planning and tax liability reduction strategies. Simpson specializes in evaluating insurance needs, assessing financial vulnerabilities and estate planning. She is one of approximately 450 African American CFPs out of the 58,000-plus worldwide, according to the College for Financial Planners Board of Standards.

Simpson provides her diverse array of clients with individualized services based on their unique financial circumstances, helping to define goals and priorities that address every need.

In 2003, she published her first book titled, *Planning for a Reason, a Season, and a Lifetime* (1stBooks Library), where she draws upon her experiences as a World Trade

Center survivor, mother and wife to encourage readers to control their finances and prepare for the unexpected.

Between 2001 and 2004, Simpson has been educating young people in several New Jersey school systems about the fundamentals of financial planning and investing. Schools in East Orange, Newark, Jersey City, and Plainfield have adopted her educational platform into their curriculum. She also works with young people through JeSEMAN Entertainment, a company her husband, Jesse, founded and named after their two children, Jesse and Emani. Through JeSEMAN's Generation X Community Association, she was actively involved in the Mayor's Youth Summit in 2002 in Jersey City, New Jersey. Simpson also offers her expertise to local churches committed to promoting economic empowerment in their congregation.

In addition to working with various community organizations, she hosts the weekly radio program "The Power of Gospel With Minister Nicole Simpson" and co-hosts, directs, produces a bi-weekly show with her husband, Jesse, "The Hot Picks @ Six and the Midday Mix," both on WRSU 88.7 FM. She also hosts "The Power Gospel Hour," a weekly television program that airs on the Cablevision leased-access stations throughout New Jersey and features profiles of people making a difference in the community. Nicole has been featured in Black Enterprise (May 2004), The Love Express (Jan. 2005), and the Newark Star-Ledger, and on UPN 9's "Black Experience," hosted by Brenda Blackmon, The Word Network, Comcast Newsmakers, Money Matters on CN8 with Lynn Doyle, Sharp Talk with Reverend Al Sharpton

BET.COM (March 2005), WRKS 98.7 and WQHT 97.1, The Doug Banks Radio Show, Bev Smith Radio Show, The Open Line and Reverend Al Sharpton's Radio Show.

Nicole participates as an advisor for an inmate driven initiative titled Women 4 Women, an organization designed to teach job certification for careers that still embrace women with a criminal record. She has hosted seminars or served as a panelist for organizations and events including the Urban Impact Summit 2006, About My Father's Business Conference 2006, Fireside Chat with Bishop Noel Jones, Megafest 2004, Hampton's Ministers Conference, Black Church Means Business Conference, the Diamonds and Pearls conference, the PSE&G Minority Exchange Regional Conference, the National Coalition of 100 Black Women (New Jersey Chapter), and the Columbia University's Get Connected Youth Conference to name a few.

Nicole stays committed to educating her community by supporting www.Blackmoneymatters.com as a contributing writer and Hope for Women magazine as a financial advisor.

Simpson lives in Union County, N.J., with her husband and two children.